HOW TO
TALK SO
YOUR
TEENAGER
WILL LISTEN

HOW TO
TALK SO
YOUR
TEENAGER
WILL LISTEN

Paul W. Swets

WORD BOOKS
PUBLISHER
WACO, TEXAS

A DIVISION OF
WORD, INCORPORATED

Library of Congress Cataloging-in-Publication Data

Swets, Paul W.
   How to talk so your teenager will listen.

   Bibliography: p.
   Includes index.
   1. Parent and child—United States. 2. Adolescent psychology—United States. 3. Communication—Psychological aspects. I. Title.
HQ755.85.S94   1988   649'.125   88-10755
ISBN 0-8499-3105-3 (pbk.)

Printed in the United States of America
89801239 AGF 987654321

To my parents,

Bill and Ethel Swets,

who not only taught me to talk and listen,
but also demonstrated the kind of communication
patterns when I was a teen that generated
continuing respect, gratitude, and love.

Contents

Foreword

Good communication with my children doesn't come easily for me. Perhaps that's one reason Paul and Jud wrote this book. They had me in mind!

When I say things that cause my son to argue or my daughter to cry, my problem is not that I don't love my children. My problem is that sometimes I don't know how to express my feelings or listen or resolve conflicts in ways that demonstrate that love.

Happily, I'm learning. This book has reduced the strain, the tension, the hurt feelings, the painful misunderstandings. It has caused my children and me to smile more often.

Talking so teenagers will listen and listening so they will talk takes work. It comes at a high price, but miscommunication costs far more. That's why you will discover passion in this book. It's not just about the mechanics of getting through to our children. Rather, it concerns preventing serious crises and increasing the opportunities for parents, whether married or single, to make a difference in the development of happy, well-rounded, morally sound, and productive teenagers.

My daughter Jessica and I count it a privilege to know the authors firsthand. They live what they write. We know Paul and Jud could not have produced such a book if they had not first proved its power in their own relationship.

Jessica is delighted this book is completed for she is eleven years old and already counting on Paul and me making the most of our best communication skills.

Janiece S. S. Swets

A Personal Invitation to Parents

Parents of teens and parents of babies have something in common. They spend a great amount of time trying to get their kids to talk.

As my son Judson became an adolescent, I wanted to find some way to keep us talking and listening. I remembered that when I was a teen, my father bought an old racing boat that needed extensive repair. We spent long hours talking and working together on that boat—a highlight of my adolescent years. With the same hopes in mind, I asked my son to work with me on this book.

On the way to the tennis courts, jogging around the block, or sprawled on the family room floor, we found the project required a lot of brainstorming and debating, giving and taking. There were times of stress, frustration, and misunderstanding, but we also experienced the victories of breaking through communication barriers and reaching mutual understanding.

In the first eleven chapters, I benefited from Jud's first-hand insights as a teenager and our discussion of each communication principle. He developed a survey designed to capture the thoughts and feelings of a broad spectrum of junior and senior high school students. Jud's chapter, "Five Messages Teens Want to Hear," is based on over 800 responses to that survey as well as his own reading and thinking.

From the survey we found that teenagers often stop talking to their parents because they fear having their ideas dismissed or discounted by two of the most important people in their lives. They fear rejection and judgmental responses if they don't say what their parents want to hear. Often the path of least resistance is to say nothing. To break through the silence barriers and encourage the free flow of ideas, skillful talking and listening by parents is required. Listening conveys acceptance, a powerful incentive for open communication. It also helps parents know how to talk so that their teenagers will want to listen.

Most parents are trying their best to raise their children. A nationwide poll in the USA revealed that people were most concerned about family, work, money, health, aging, and managing their time. However, at the top of the list of major concerns was the family.[1] The family is what we make it—and making it work is our number one goal.

It is not working as well as it could. Even with the best of intentions, communication between parents and teens often ends up in argument, yelling, misunderstanding, and psychological distance. The result is that our teens feel left out, put down, and cut off from the very persons who are most significant to them. Neither parents nor teenagers want it this way. Our survey reveals that teens want to talk to their parents about many things. Both want family closeness but they don't know how to bridge the gap.

Can we increase the number of times we get through to our teens? Can we learn the necessary skills? Can we change our attitudes, our choice of words, our very selves? Yes! *Effective communication on a consistent basis is possible.* We can't control what our teens say and think. But we can control ourselves—what we say and how we say it—and that may be enough to win the battle for understanding.

When our communication fails, it is because we are making a limited number of errors. We say and do a few things wrong. Anyone can reduce the errors and increase the quality of relationships. *You* can do it. Each of the twelve chapters in this book focuses on a major problem parents face in communicating with their teens and shows how to solve these problems. In most cases, dramatic changes are not necessary. Even slight adjustments in modes of listening and talking can produce major benefits in parent/teen communication.

If while reading this book you sense occasional repetition, it is a good sign that you are assimilating the concepts well. Deliberate and progressive repetition is built in because it allows our minds to apply concepts more accurately and in a greater number of situations. At the end of each chapter, "Action Steps for Positive Communication" guide us in applying the principles and skills that have been discussed.

Jud and I enjoyed writing this book. We tested the principles and found they not only helped us to talk and listen skillfully to each other, but also enabled us to know the satisfaction of staying in touch, the joy of being understood and appreciated. We invite you to experience the same.

When your fifteen-year-old son does speak, he often says one of two things: either "Okay," which, as we know, means "I haven't killed anyone," or "No problem."

Bill Cosby, *Fatherhood*[1]

Communicating with Teens—Super Challenge

Communicating with teenagers would lack challenge if we didn't have to interpret every "Okay" and investigate each "No problem."

"What did your teacher say when you told her you didn't have your term paper ready?"

"Okay."

"I saw the police in front of your school today. What happened?"

"No problem."

Listening so that teenagers will talk and talking so that they will listen is like participating in a basketball game. Players have to know certain skills to get the ball to the goal. No problem . . . except for the opponents. The opponents are *not* our teens, but are such obstacles to communicating as time pressures, frustrations, preoccupations, past failures, and a feeling of hopelessness. When we know what to do and how to do it, we can overcome these opponents and achieve the goals of:

— knowing what our teens think and feel
— gaining mutual respect
— sharing interests
— developing better rapport
— enjoying increasing cooperation
— reducing frustration
— experiencing a more peaceful, relaxed atmosphere in the home.

WHAT'S A PARENT TO DO?

When teens try to make us feel that everything that goes wrong is our fault, when they clam up and walk out of the room—perhaps the way we used to do—we might feel like failures as parents, but we must not give up!

In my counseling I have seen both parents and teens completely frustrated with the other, but where there was a desire for healing and a will to build a strong relationship, even though one-sided at first, frustration eventually gave way to gratitude that they never gave up the struggle.

DEVELOPING A PERSPECTIVE

What characteristics does the term *teenager* bring to your mind? Forgetful? Arrogant? Rude? Irresponsible? Insensitive? Scatterbrained? Unpredictable? Selfish? Perhaps teens are all of these at various times, but this age group can also be delightful. They can feel deeply the pain or joy of others. They can be humorous, spontaneous, creative, caring, spunky, thoughtful, and fun-loving. At times, they may be mature beyond their years, yet youthful enough to dream and to reach for the stars. Being with them keeps us fresh and in tune with the future.

I remember that when my son Judson was an infant, I thought of him as a bundle of energy eager to be released, as an artistic masterpiece in the process of formation. Consequently, I treated him with great care and respect. Now that he is a teenager I realize that the image I have of my son still colors what I say and how I say it. It also influences the development of his self-concept. If I call him a loser, he will tend to act like a loser. If I treat him as a winner, he will be more apt to act like a winner. Since teens are in the vulnerable process of identity formation, *how we think of them and what we tell them they are influences what they will become.*

In one of our surveys, Cheryl (15) wrote:

> The way my mom talks to me makes me feel great, like an adult. She respects me and my feelings just as I do hers. On the other hand, my stepdad makes me feel like hitting him, or running away sometimes just to escape his hurting words. I wish he could learn to treat me with respect.

When teens show their worst selves to us, we can bring out the best in them by showing our best selves. If we can talk skillfully and listen intently to them, we create opportunities to build respect, to bridge troubled waters. Of course, the bridge can not be built in a day. It takes time, patience, persistence, commitment, love, and skill. But isn't that what parenting is about?

TRAINED—NOT BLAMED

In addition to learning grammar, vocabulary, and writing, some of us may have had courses in public speaking. But how many of us were trained in listening techniques? How many of us were trained in responding to strong emotions, in resolving conflicts, and in the art of talking to our children so that they will want to talk to us? This lack of training often results in communication breakdown, followed by blaming ourselves as well as our children.

Blame produces guilt feelings. It demotivates, deflates, and depresses. Self-blame is like putting on a shirt made of coarse hair, the way the monks used to do. It is futile to punish ourselves for communication failures. Training can help to erase self-blame by helping us know what to avoid, what to aim for, and how to make changes necessary to reach our positive parenting goals.

The Sperry Corporation discovered that by training employees in listening skills, they could decrease communication error and save millions of dollars. Research showed that those who had been trained in listening techniques became more highly motivated, made fewer mistakes, and enjoyed their work more than those who did not receive the training.

The benefits of training are available to us. As we apply the communication principles in each chapter, we can enjoy the advantages of being trained—not blamed.

You Can Count on You

Although we cannot always count on our teenagers to do what we want them to do, we can count on ourselves to take the following five steps toward better communicating because each is an action we can control.

We can make slight adjustments. When things go wrong in communicating with our teens, as they undoubtedly will, we can review what happened and make any changes that are necessary. While big adjustments in what we say and how we say it might overwhelm us, slight adjustments are more manageable. Even small differences in tone of voice, choice of words, facial expressions, or the way we listen can alter teens' views of us and their responses to us.

In October of 1984, my family was invited by NASA to the John F. Kennedy Space Center to watch the launch and landing of the space shuttle Challenger. We were there because David Leestma, my cousin, was one of the astronauts aboard the space shuttle. It was a thrilling and spectacular sight to see the 200,000-pound Challenger, after 133 orbits and many slight adjustments during the 4.3 million miles of travel, land precisely on target. Words between parents and teens also can be on target when our aim is clear and we are willing to make slight adjustments as needed.

We can set communication goals. Here are some examples that help me. My goals are to:

— think before I speak
— listen without interrupting
— avoid a judgmental tone of voice
— speak calmly without raising my voice
— ask questions that promote interesting conversation
— talk to my teen the way I want my teen to talk to me.

If our goal is to encourage, but our habit is to berate, our goal will help us gain a new mind set, a predisposition to respond in a positive way. We can enhance the goal by recording the ratio of compliments to criticisms within a certain time period. We can actually *count* our progress. Communication goals help us to know what adjustments to make and when to make them. They set our minds on a clear track, focus our attention, and provide a target at which to aim.

We can choose our words. When we keep our goals in mind during our conversations, we choose our words accordingly. Without goals, choice of words is left to whim, to the feelings of the moment. The word choices below are simple, but the difference our choices produce in attitude and relationship over a period of time can be profound.

Choice 1	*Choice 2*
Daughter: Do you know where my shoes are?	Daughter: Do you know where my shoes are?
Parent: You never put them away. That's why you are always losing them!	Parent: I believe you left them by the blue chair.
Daughter: O yeah? Why are you always losing your keys?	Daughter: Thanks, Mom.

In choice 1 the parent reacts to the daughter's question with a judgmental statement, attempts to correct a behavior, and generates hassle. In choice 2 the parent responds without judgment and generates gratitude. The word choices we make in conversation determine the quality and depth of our relationships and are completely within our control.

We can draw upon our native knowledge. Reflect for a moment on the time when you were an adolescent. Can you remember some of the struggles you endured socially, physically, and emotionally? Can you recall what your parents said to you that helped and what hurt? Can you think of some of the mistakes you vowed never to make when you became a parent?

This book is designed to help you remember what you already know about teenagers because you and I have a whole reservoir of information buried in our subconscious minds. From our memory banks we can recall how we felt when adults talked to us with respect, or yelled at us in disgust, or asked us how we felt about some matter, or complimented us on jobs well done. That recall, combined with new insights and fresh skills, will help us to meet a super challenge—communicating with our teenagers.

We can commit ourselves to making the most of our best. I like the way Harry Emerson Fosdick put it: "Have the daring to accept yourself as a bundle of possibilities and undertake the game of making the most of your best."[2] It may well be that you have some fear about learning new communication skills and trying to develop new habits. Most of us do. We are afraid of trying something difficult and falling on our faces. The only way for us to conquer that fear is to put our hearts into learning these skills and discover what really is our best.

Author and speech expert, Dorothy Sarnoff, tells an old and charming story of a little girl who watched a sculptor as he started work on a fresh block of marble. Some weeks later, the child returned and saw that a lion was taking shape. Astonished, the little girl tilted her head to one side and asked, "Did you know all the time that there was a lion inside?"[3]

As you read this book and apply what you learn, you may find that the principles of artful communication are like a hammer and chisel. They will help you discover the piece of art you really are deep inside.

I believe there is a better self inside each of us that can make a positive difference in the way we communicate with our teenagers. How do we find it? By committing ourselves to making the most of our best. Without commitment, we will give up when we fail. With commitment, when we fail (and we will at times), we will adjust, try again, and eventually succeed.

A SELF-INVENTORY

One of the great tasks which precedes success in any area of human endeavor is, as the oracle at Delphi said, to "know thyself." What are our strengths and weaknesses as communicators? We may have a vague idea of some new directions in which we would like to go, but we really "can't get there from here" if we don't know where "here" is.

The following inventory can help determine where you are now in your skill development and where you may need to make adjustments. With an attitude that you have nothing to lose and perhaps a great deal to gain, have fun with these questions. Circle the number that best represents the frequency of each item in your experience (1 = seldom, 2 = sometimes, 3 = often, 4 = usually).

1 2 3 4   1. My teenager listens to what I say.

1 2 3 4   2. When communication breaks down, I adjust what I say and how I say it and try again.

1 2 3 4   3. When I talk with my teen, I keep in mind the developmental characteristics of adolescence.

1 2 3 4   4. I ask questions and make statements that help my teen through the various areas of adolescent development.

1 2 3 4   5. I earn the right to be heard.

1 2 3 4   6. In emotional situations, I think of the consequences of my words before I speak.

1 2 3 4   7. I listen to my teen at least as much as I talk.

1 2 3 4   8. My teen talks to me about his or her feelings and problems.

1 2 3 4   9. When communication breaks down, I understand why.

1 2 3 4   10. I repair communication breakdowns.

1 2 3 4   11. I respond effectively when my teen is angry.

1 2 3 4   12. I defend myself verbally against attacks in a way that promotes understanding.

1 2 3 4   13. When necessary, I confront and say *no* to my teen without losing my temper.

1 2 3 4   14. I discipline my teen in a way that wins respect.

1 2 3 4   15. I am aware of how my temperament influences communication with my teen.

1 2 3 4   16. In matters of discipline, I give a consistent message to my teen.

1 2 3 4   17. I am conscious of the major problems teenagers face.

1 2 3 4   18. I help my teen figure out ways to meet these problems successfully.

1 2 3 4   19. When conflict arises, I follow a clear plan
                 for trying to resolve it.
1 2 3 4   20. In the midst of a conflict, I state my views
                 calmly.
1 2 3 4   21. I talk to my teen about life's major decisions.
1 2 3 4   22. I model the kinds of choices I want my teen
                 to make.
1 2 3 4   23. I know the messages my teen wants to hear
                 from me as a parent.
1 2 3 4   24. I communicate these messages to my teen.

How did you do? Would you like to find out? Determine your score by adding each of the numbers you circled; then check your total points with the following guide:

92–96 Super	In fact, your score might be "incredible." Would your teen rate you approximately the same on each of these items? If so, you need not read on. Give this book to a friend.
78–91 Good	You are on track. You have a grasp of some basic communication skills. Keep going and refine them for even greater success.
50–77 Fair	You are missing some of the joy of communication with your teen. If you want to make some changes and experience success, you can. Remember that even small changes can produce great gains.
24–49 Poor	Relax! Maybe you are being too hard on yourself. Keep in mind that you might not be responsible for how your teen responds to you. If communication is bad, it might not be your fault. You are responsible for yourself and what you can control.

ACTION STEPS FOR POSITIVE COMMUNICATION

Each chapter ends with Action Steps to help us think through the information in the chapter, apply the information to our situations, and take positive control of our communication behavior. When we act on an idea, we make it our own; each time it becomes easier to apply more often.

1. Since motives are the backbone of any commitment, why do you want better communication between you and your teenager?

2. What are some obstacles you and your teen have experienced that interfere with good communication?

3. When obstacles do arise, what can you do to get around them?

4. As you review the Self-Inventory, on what skills did you score low? Put check marks in front of skills you want to improve.

5. Focus attention now on *one* of the skills you checked and write a communication goal related to it. For example, "My goal is to learn a clear plan for conflict resolution" or "My goal is to listen to my teen in such a way that he/she will enjoy talking to me." Your goal may seem like a small step, but it can be very significant to the quality of your relationship with your teen. It's a step in the right direction.

> Young people need a sense of "growing,"
> of being in a process of transition.
>
> David Elkind,
> *All Grown Up and No Place to Go*[1]

A Quick View of Adolescence

Dad, you've got to remember that I'm just a kid. It's hard for me to remember everything. I'll grow out of this. It just takes time.

Jud Swets at age 12

Adolescents are neither miniature adults nor children. They are in transition from something relatively fixed toward something not yet clear. Their changes occur too fast for us to paint their portraits. Snapshots are needed, for one moment they act like children, the next minute like adults, then somewhere in-between. If we want to gain a realistic view of them, we need to accept as normal some blur and smudge, some times of inconsistency and misunderstanding. And we need patience, for this growing up transition "just takes time."

WHAT IS AN ADOLESCENT?

No couple embraces and says, "Let's have an adolescent!" If that were part of the process, there might be a lot fewer of us.

Fortunately, we do have several years to prepare for the risk and excitement of parenting adolescents. Yet, many parents tell me that they don't feel ready. They discover that the difference between raising children and raising adolescents is more than age; it's a whole new ballgame in which the old rules don't always apply and the new goal lines are uncertain.

What is adolescence? It's a time of transition roughly equivalent to the teenage years, but often extending beyond them in both directions. Adolescence is defined as the period between the onset of puberty (sexual maturation) and the attainment of full adulthood (when one is self supporting and legally responsible for one's actions). It is a time of major development physically, socially, mentally, emotionally, morally, and spiritually. It is that dramatic passage from one stage to another in which everything about our teens is both fascinating and confounding—to us and to them.

In the course of the last one hundred years, the duration of adolescence has lengthened due to earlier sexual maturation and later periods of self-support. Often this prolonged stage produces turbulent emotions and conflicting messages. Adolescents want independence, but can't afford it. They want to risk the dangers of an adult world, but they also want the security of being able to come home. They may be ready for marriage sexually, but not financially. Their bodies say "Go!", but their bank accounts say "No!"

This waiting has a positive side. Psychologist Erik H. Erikson characterizes adolescence as "a psycho-social moratorium on adulthood"[2] which provides young people with an extended period of time to develop their identity as adults. Ideally, this moratorium provides time to explore, to laugh, to make mistakes, to start over again, to learn what life is about. Yet, in recent years the "moratorium on adulthood" is in danger of vanishing. Professor David Elkind reveals that today's social pressures place adult demands on teenagers without giving them adequate time and the tools to respond. The result is stress and related symptoms: drastic increases in drug and alcohol abuse, crime, psychological withdrawal, and even suicide among teenagers.[3]

Parents can help reduce stress by listening actively and demonstrating sensitivity to the developing world of their children. In fact, adolescence offers us a *second chance* to communicate with teenagers. They are breaking out of childish habits of thoughts and entering a realm that is qualitatively different. It's confusing, exciting, and scary. Teenagers sense that they need information and support from us to survive. If we exercise good communication skills, we will gain opportunities to demonstrate to our teens that, when needed, parents really can lift some of a teen's burdens and share some adventures too.

Can you remember the embarrassment, the awkward moments, the failures, and the successes you experienced as a teenager? Although conditions today are not the same as when we were teens, some of the problems of our teens are similar. The value of this chapter in understanding our teenagers will be enhanced if we can draw upon our "native knowledge" and reflect on our physical, social, mental, emotional, moral, and spiritual experiences during adolescence.

PHYSICAL DEVELOPMENT

Sexual characteristics, voice quality, body shape, coordination, appetite, weight, and height are all in the process of increased alteration. Since personal identity is strongly related to physical appearance, some teenagers experience what psychologist Erik Erikson calls "identity confusion." They may not be sure who they are or who they want to be from one day to the next. Mood swings related to hormonal changes often are dramatic. A facial blemish can ruin a whole month of compliments. Sometimes the growth process makes teens feel more tired than adults and decreases their ability to respond effectively to frustrations and tensions. At other times, their energy seems boundless.

It's not easy to talk with adolescents about physical concerns, especially sex. It's awkward for them and us. But they worry a lot about their bodies, their rate of development, how they compare with their peers, and whether or not they are "normal." Crawford, 13, wrote to us that he wished he could talk to his parents about *girls*. "I don't understand them! What do they do? I want to know truthfully why they aren't hovering about me. Is it my personality or am I just invisible to them?"

Teens need us to be available to answer their questions.

For lack of a better word, they want us to be "askable." That means that we will be most effective when we don't preach, pry, or probe. An "askable" parent listens carefully and answers briefly.

Strategies

• Be prepared to provide accurate information and clear values regarding sex. Give them a good book on sexual development to supplement what you tell them. (See the resource section in the back of the book for suggestions.) Help them to see the sexual relationship as a positive and beautiful experience within marriage.

• Never joke about physical characteristics such as height and weight. Psychologist Bruce Narramore writes in *Adolescence Is Not an Illness,* "Some parents attempt to motivate their children through sarcasm or ridicule. They believe teasing or pressuring teens about excess weight or untidiness will force positive changes. But these pressure tactics only create resentment and strong resistance."[4]

• Treat delicate topics with great sensitivity. If a daughter's first menstruation catches her (and you) unexpectedly and she panics, let her express her fear and reassure her with accurate information and a positive attitude. Help her to view it as a marvel, something to celebrate, a rite of passage.

• Think and talk about wellness, not sickness. It is a mistake to shower our teens with attention, affection, and our time only when they are not feeling well. The message we need to convey to our daughters is that a period is not the end of the world. We need to help our sons realize that scrapes and bruises are no big deal. Emphasize getting well. Braving aches and pains without drawing undue attention to them is a big deal. Health is something to celebrate. Wellness is a goal worth achieving. As with most everything in parenting, a positive attitude about physical health is caught, not taught. But especially with young adolescents, the "catching" can be reinforced with comments like these:

— I appreciate the fact that you exercise. I can see the results in your muscle tone.

— The way you restrained your desire for sweets and ate a balanced meal today shows a lot of self-discipline. I'm proud of you.
— Your cold is over already. It's amazing how quickly your body recovered.
— I know you had some pain today, but you went to school anyway. The way you conquer pain impresses me.

SOCIAL DEVELOPMENT

Do you remember the intensity of social alliances during adolescence? Although parental influence may still have underlying strength, on the surface and with increasing depth, the significant others in the lives of teens are their peers. Teens listen intently to whatever they sense will affect their social relationships. To some degree they are self-centered, for adolescents spend a great amount of energy trying to understand themselves and be accepted by their social environment.

Teens often give the impression that the whole world revolves around them and they seem surprised when others don't recognize this fact. I remember that as a teen I taped a card to my mirror which read, "It's monotonous to be great without anyone noticing it." My son has the following cartoon above his desk.[5]

By permission of Johnny Hart and NAS, Inc.

One morning my wife said, "Jud, I love you." He responded, "I don't blame you." We decided that we liked that response because it suggested an ego strength that can cushion painful social experiences when they come.

Some social learning is painful. In fact, according to psychologist David Elkind, teens often face social changes and conditions that are entirely unexpected and for which they are unprepared. He writes: "In many respects moving from the culture of childhood to the culture of adolescence is like moving from one society to another; and the change in behavior and conduct the adolescent encounters can lead to a form of shock—peer shock."[6]

Elkind describes three forms of peer shock. First, the shock of *exclusion*. In childhood, friendships are often determined by who lives nearby. Among teenagers, however, group membership is usually determined by fads, clubs, and cliques. It is a painful experience to feel on the "outside," not to be invited to a party, or worse, to throw a party and have no one come.

Second, the shock of *betrayal*. Children build friendships based on mutual trust and loyalty. During adolescence, relationships become more complex. Teens may find that they have been used or manipulated by another "friend" to gain some advantage for that person. This pattern occurs when teenagers are led on by members of the opposite sex. A boy may profess love and devotion to a girl in order to take advantage of her sexually and later tell his friends that she is a "tramp." In experiences of exploitation, teenagers become painfully aware of the shock of misplaced trust and betrayed loyalty.

Third, the shock of *disillusion*. Children normally accept their friends pretty much as they are, warts and all. But with puberty, they begin to idealize each other. Boys and girls who may have held each other in contempt as children now find the opposite sex interesting to look at and be around. Especially in romantic relationships, teenagers imagine the other person to be more than he or she is. The person on whom they have a "crush" seems perfect in every way. But these crushes don't last long because soon the reality of the human being sets in; they are shocked to find flaws in appearance, character, values, or irritating personal habits.

When social shocks are combined with the other stresses of adolescence, teenagers face a complex array of pressures and learning tasks. They need parents who can serve as buffers and guides.

Strategies

• Communicate. This means that we listen when our teens are willing to talk and ask questions or make statements that help them make wise decisions regarding social relationships.

— I like it that Aaron talks with you so easily and seems to have a great sense of humor.
— How would you describe a true friend?
— I still remember a friend I had in high school. He was easy to talk to. He always seemed to be there when I needed him. I could trust him.
— It can be a painful experience when "friends" let you down.

The goal is to keep the lines of communication open so that our teens feel they can come to us at any time with their questions or concerns.

• Be patient. Although solutions to our teens' social problems may be readily apparent to us, we need to allow them time to grasp the complexity of their problems and learn how to solve them.

• Stay objective. We need to be careful what we say about their friends. Because our teens' friends are so much a part of their lives, our teens may view any verbal attack on their friends as an attack on them. If we disapprove of their friends, we need to have good reasons and remain as objective as possible in presenting them (e.g., avoid labeling and unfair criticism).

• Encourage healthy social exposure. We can volunteer to entertain our teens' friends at our homes and support supervised group activities, especially for young teens. This will help to broaden their social skills and prepare them for formal dating when they are older.

• Clarify expectations. We will likely need to talk about principles and set clear limits about dating and curfew that were unnecessary before. But we need to maintain a positive attitude about this side of adolescent experience. We will get along better and exert more influence if our teens get the impression that we are for them, not against them.

• Model resistance to peer pressure. We face it too, don't we? At her 93rd birthday party, one grand woman stated that "the best thing about being over 90 is that you outgrow peer pressure!" Until that time comes for us, we all face the pressure to conform. We can help our teens by our own example (choosing directions we want to take rather than letting ourselves be pressured into something against our better judgment) and by building our teens' confidence in their right to assert themselves when their values run counter to the crowd.

MENTAL DEVELOPMENT

Adolescents begin to think at a new level. From ancient times a child of six or seven was thought to have entered the age of reason, for at that age children begin to use logic. Psychologist Jean Piaget claimed that after childhood, a second stage of reasoning ability appears in adolescence which he called "formal operations"—the ability to deal with possibilities, to think abstractly, to enjoy simile and metaphor, satire and parody.[7]

My wife Janiece and I recognized Jud's new level of thinking in early adolescence. He began to argue, debate, negotiate, and test ideas. We learned that when Jud took the opposite side on any point of discussion, he was not necessarily trying to put us down, make us feel bad, or reject our ideas. He was simply trying to shape his own mental identity or exercise his new thinking capacity. One night during our evening meal, he asked, "What would happen to the rotation of the earth if all the people on the earth began walking in the same direction at the same time?" Then, after a minute of silence, he said, "Dad, you haven't answered my question." I replied, "I'm still trying to imagine it!"

Strategies

• Encourage mental development. Listening to our teens' ideas does not necessarily mean that we agree with them, but it conveys the message that we think their ideas are important. That encourages them to continue talking and thinking. In the process, they often sort out false ideas themselves and come to a clearer understanding of what really is important to them.

• Ask questions. Keep in mind the three conditions or 3 C's of asking good questions: *cues* that our teens are willing to talk, a *context* that is informal, such as when we are doing something or going somewhere together, and *content* which is upbeat rather than heavy. It is much better to ask a few key questions than it is to know all of the answers.

• Talk as a friend. Talk about ideas and feelings that are important to us much like we would to our friends. Work toward a mutual dialogue that is honest and reflective. One sixteen-year-old girl in our survey wrote: "I am able to talk with my parents openly about almost anything. My mom is so terrific because she manages to see my side of the situation even when she doesn't agree with me. When she's wrong, she admits it. When she's right, she takes the time to explain why."

• Allow harmless overstatement. A teen's thinking is still pretty much in flux. Refrain from reacting to rash statements or a know-it-all tone of voice. It takes time, experience, and education to realize how much one really doesn't know. If my son were to say that my political views are hopelessly out of date, there is no need for me to get angry or defensive. I simply need to remember the idealism of youth and that when I said such things as a teen, I wanted to be taken seriously. I could say, "Son, you make some very good points. I admit that I certainly don't know all that I would like to know. Perhaps my views will change someday . . . and maybe yours will too. (Smile) But at this point in my life, this is how I view the situation."

EMOTIONAL DEVELOPMENT

At times we feel teenagers are on an emotional roller coaster—one moment riding high on a burst of confidence, optimism, and fun-loving play, and the next plummeting to the depths of insecurity, pessimism, and depression. While to us these ups and downs may be senseless, to our teens they are real even though they may not be able to give us "reasons" for what they feel.

When a teenager explodes, "You don't understand!" the

reason may be that our teens don't know the words to describe a feeling and we aren't very good at guessing. Difficult as it is, one of the tasks of understanding adolescence is to discover the *reasons of the heart,* to learn what teens are feeling and why. The process of talking about feelings in a nonjudgmental context will help teens gain control over fluctuating moods and how they express their feelings.

It ought to be clear to us, perhaps painfully so, that we can't expect our teens to express their feelings better than our own day-to-day example. We know from experience that healthy expression of emotions is a learning process that takes time. It works best in an environment that allows room for differences in temperament and encourages fresh starts. We can't fulfill this task of emotional development for our teens, but we can talk and listen in ways that help instead of hinder.

Strategies

• Model healthy expression of feeling. By identifying our feelings as well as we can, our teens learn the vocabulary of feelings. We can exercise control as we talk about our own struggles.

—When the boss makes me stay overtime at work, I feel very frustrated. It's hard for me to know how to express my feelings in a way he will understand and that doesn't get me fired.
—When you don't come home at the time we agreed upon, I feel very concerned about your safety. On top of that I feel angry because I assume you probably forgot to call me.

• Don't minimize feelings. "Cheer up. That's nothing to get upset about" is not helpful. On top of feeling bad the teen is challenged to defend why the feeling is as strong as it is. Having to do this makes the teen think the adult is insensitive and further communication is likely to be cut off.

• Don't overreact to emotional lows or highs. Adolescents need freedom and time to gain emotional balance. Learning to feel deeply and strongly is a significant part of a fully functioning human being. If our teens can learn to express feelings in a healthy manner and avoid the really damaging side of emotions (the release of feelings in words or actions that hurt another person), they will have accomplished one of the significant tasks of adolescence.

• Enjoy times of high humor. Our family loves to laugh about everyday foibles, like what Nellie did the first time we took her to the Vet or how I almost spilled a glass of ice water on the lap of Jud's girlfriend the first time we met her. Joining in the hilarity can heighten our teens' sense that we appreciate them. It provides ballast for the turbulent times.

• Celebrate achievement. Unfortunately, sometimes we empathize better with defeats than victories. But times of exuberance and optimism need to be reinforced and shared as much as possible. I will never forget the thrill of hearing Jud's campaign speech when he ran for president of his senior class . . . and he won't forget that we were there to experience the excitement with him. That night we went out for dinner to celebrate his victory. One man at the restaurant leaned over and said, "You must be very proud of your son." I replied, "Yes, I am. But I would be just as proud of him if he had not won." I hope Jud won't forget that either.

MORAL/SPIRITUAL DEVELOPMENT

In healthy families, parents are not afraid to talk about their values and faith with their children. Dolores Curran, in *Traits of a Healthy Family,* writes that in a survey that asked 551 professionals to rank a list of fifty-six possible characteristics of a healthy family, the trait "teaches a sense of right and wrong" was ranked seven and "a shared religious core" was ranked ten.[8]

In spite of the importance of these two traits, educators and clinical psychologists report that some children grow up in a moral and spiritual vacuum. When parents' moral codes and beliefs are a confusing blend of the ten commandments, social custom, and self-interest, it adversely affects the moral development of their teenagers. Psychologist David Elkind writes: "Teenagers need a clearly defined value system against which to test other values and discover their own. But when the important adults in their lives don't know what their own values are and are not sure what is right and what is wrong, what is good and what is bad, the teenagers' task is even more difficult."[9] Elkind indicates that ambivalence on the part of the parent is likely to be interpreted as license by the teenager. When a parent says "I don't know what's right," the teenager hears "I don't care what you do."

The alternative to ambivalence is not dogmatic rigidity, but a clear commitment to a system of values we believe is right and that will promote healthy moral development in our teens. Most teens want to know what their parents believe.

Dr. Robert Coles, teacher, research psychiatrist, and Pulitzer prize-winning author from Harvard, emphasizes the point that there is a developing moral sense within a child.

> I happen to think it is God-given, that there is a craving for a moral order. I would say the child has a need for "moral articulation" of what the world is all about, what it means, and what this life is about. This desire to figure out the world, to make sense of it, and in some way find meaning in life is built into each of us . . . . These questions are connected to one's nature as a human being.[10]

Clearly it is best to guide the process of moral development in our children at an early age. But due to the developing need of teenagers to make ethical decisions, adolescence does provide us with a second chance to listen and talk about moral and spiritual matters.

Strategies

• Clarify your own moral code and religious beliefs. We can't give away what we don't have.

• Avoid a condescending attitude or judgmental tone of voice. When teenagers seem to reject their parents' religious views, the problem may not be the moral code or beliefs, but *how* they are communicated. When youth specialist Jay Kesler spoke to a convention of 12,000 young people, he wondered if he could say anything about sexual morality that would be accepted by these teens. His speech was well received. One seventeen-year-old girl summed up the reason why: "I was trying to figure out why I am not offended when you say some of the same things my folks say. I think it's that you don't talk *down* to us or *at* us. You always say "we" rather than "you" when talking about our problems."[11]

• Do what you say. Teens are quick to spot hypocrisy. This doesn't mean that we have to pretend to be perfect parents. No one is. But it does mean that we strive to act according to our values.

• Admit mistakes. There is nothing worse or more foolish than a parent who presumes to be perfect or appears self-righteous. Our teens know us too well. On the other hand, there is nothing more persuasive about the rightness of our standards when we admit we have failed to live up to our standards and say, "I'm sorry. I was wrong."

• Talk about what you believe. Teenagers have told me that they don't really know what their parents believe about God or the meaning of life. Yet, perhaps more than at any other time, these beliefs become important to the teen as reference points in decision-making and behavior.

• Don't force-feed religion. In an article on the problem of runaways, Dr. Norman Vincent Peale wrote, "The knowledge and love of God are life's greatest joy and privilege, but they can't be forced or hammered into anyone."[12] Teenagers are attracted to what works. If they see that our faith gives us confidence to face problems, that forgiveness really is experienced and practiced, that our relationship to God fills our lives with joy and meaning, then sooner or later they will want the same.

THE "WELL-ROUNDED" ADOLESCENT

It is helpful to have a clear image of what a "well-rounded" adolescent might look like in terms of the five developmental areas discussed in this chapter. It will give us the full picture and help us to know what we are aiming at.

If we use the spokes in a wheel to represent each of the five developmental areas, it is clear that when one or more areas are not developed, the wheel will not go around. Progress requires well-rounded development.

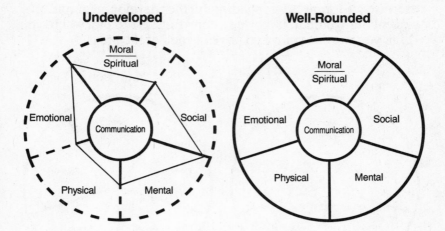

Keep in mind that it is normal for the wheel to be out of round at different stages of the teen's development. No one develops at the same rate or in the same way, and it is important not to try to hurry the developmental process.

Communication is the hub supporting the spokes of well-rounded development. It is always at the center of a healthy, growing relationship. In the following chapters we will focus on how to increase our communication skills so that we can make the most of the best times with our teenagers and minimize the effect of the worst times.

ACTION STEPS FOR POSITIVE COMMUNICATION

1. Try to remember what it was like for you as a teenager. How did your parents communicate with you? How did you want them to communicate with you?

2. In which of the five developmental areas do you think your teen needs the most support? What can you say or do that will give your teen that support?

3. On the two circles that follow, plot where you think you are and where your teen is in each of the five areas by putting a dot on the line between 0 and 5. Then connect the dots. This

exercise will show areas needing further development and special encouragement. It may be interesting also to plot where you think you were at your teen's age in each of the areas.

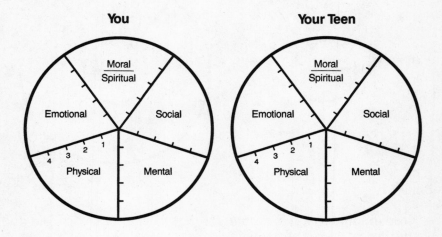

Dad, it would be helpful to me if you would look at me instead of the paper when we are talking. We could finish our conversation quicker.

Jud Swets at age 13

Getting through to Teens

Why is it so hard to get through to teens? Could it be for some of the same reasons teens have a hard time getting through to us? One of the most common complaints from teenagers is that although they want to communicate with their parents, they are turned off by what their parents say and how they say it. Or, as in my case, by the way they don't listen.

Sometimes we do get through. We say the right thing in a way that is heard. We take the attitude that if someone has to take the first step, we will. As a result, we experience less stress, more heart-to-heart talks, and greater appreciation of the best qualities we are trying to instill in our teens.

The following five steps will lead us past most conversation barriers and keep us close. They will direct us toward our teens even during such turbulence of adolescent development as hormonal imbalance, the feeling of not measuring up, or a boyfriend/girlfriend problem that short-circuits all other relationships.

1. Earning the Right to Be Heard

In an interview with journalist Ann McCarroll, fifteen-year-old Bob said that he had "some mother!" He explained:

Each morning she sits with me while I eat breakfast. We talk about anything and everything. She isn't refined or elegant or educated. She's a terrible housekeeper. She uses double negatives. But she's interested in everything I do and she listens to me—even if she's busy or tired.[1]

Spending time, showing interest, listening, talking about "anything and everything"—this is behavior that wins the right to be heard. It's adapting to the interests and attitudes of teenagers as Bob's mother did. It's really not all that hard if we commit to it by mentally putting ourselves into teen situations as fully as possible. We can ask ourselves:

— What activities/experiences is my teen involved in?
— How does my teen feel about these involvements?
— How can I best draw out my teen's thoughts and feelings?
— What concerns do we really need to talk about?

Such an exercise on our part can generate a surprising number of ideas to discuss and questions to ask that will show our genuine interest.

In addition, we need to *really listen.* We will have to discipline ourselves to focus on our teens, not ourselves. This is not the time to argue or counter every comment with our ideas. It is the time to use the "mutual exchange" principle. As children we may have used that principle this way: "If you hit me, I'll hit you back!" In winning the right to be heard, the mutual exchange principle works this way: "If I genuinely listen, I create the atmosphere in which my teen is most likely to listen to me."

"But I never seem to get equal time," you say. That may be true for most parent-teen communication. Due to the nature of developing adolescents, they need to spend an inordinate amount of time keeping track of their thoughts, feelings, schedules, and what's happening in the lives of their peers.

That takes an enormous amount of mental energy. The full measure of respect and response we hope for from our teens comes gradually.

A common mistake we parents make is to think that we can buy the right to be heard with money or gifts. It doesn't work. Teens need our continuing love and attention. When they experience it through our willingness to genuinely listen, then we win the right to be heard.

2. DEVELOPING A CLEAR PURPOSE

We all slip up in what we say because the tongue tends to function without purpose or direction. It's like a blazing forest fire, a ship without a rudder, a restless stallion without a bridle.[2] Words fly out of our mouths without our considering their effect. The pay-off for lashing out may be a feeling of temporary relief. But at what cost? Terrible damage can be done when we speak without a clearly defined purpose.

Purpose is a controlling device. It's like a bridle or a rudder. If the purpose is positive, then in spite of negative emotions or stormy circumstances, our purpose in communication can prevail and often control an unruly tongue. According to writer Norman Cousins, "Effective communications, oral or written, depend absolutely on a clear understanding of one's purpose. That purpose should be clearly identified."[3]

As I reflect on this statement, I realize that I do have some very clear communication goals that guide what I say to my son and how I say it. I don't always follow them, but I know that I would slip up a lot more without the following goals to guide me:

1. To speak to my son in such a way that his self-esteem is enhanced, causing him to feel good about himself and to have the confidence that he can solve his problems.
2. To listen to my son in such a way that he knows that I care enough to understand him.
3. To let him know that what he says and how he feels is important to me, even when I disagree.
3. To achieve mutual understanding through honest feedback.

4. To communicate my concerns about any negative behavior with firmness, but without putdowns and recriminations.
5. To send a clear message to my son that I love him, that his well-being is as important to me as my own.

Walking beside my teen through his period of adolescence is too important a journey for me not to have constantly in mind clear destinations and self-directing goals that help me break through the barriers.

3. AVOIDING CONVERSATION KILLERS

Conversations with our teens may be going along perfectly well when, without notice, they end abruptly. A "conversation killer" could be the culprit. Although sometimes disguised, these killers usually can be identified by one or more of the following characteristics: incessant talking, contradictions, putdowns, dogmatic statements, a judgmental tone of voice, unfair generalizations, and responses that reveal one has not listened. For example:

— No, it cost $5.50, not $4.50.
— Hey dummy, what did I just tell you to do?
— You idiot!
— Teenagers are terrible drivers.
— When will you grow up?

To avoid killing a conversation, check yourself on each of the following questions by circling *Yes* or *No*.

Yes No   Do I talk longer than a minute without giving my teen a chance to speak? (Time yourself.)

Yes No   Do I talk about myself or my interests without spending at least as much time listening to my teen's interests?

Yes No   Do I correct or contradict on nonessential matters when I think my teen's ideas are wrong?

Yes No   Do I assume that getting the facts straight is more important than understanding feelings?

Yes No   Do I call my teen names that, regardless of my intention, could be interpreted as uncomplimentary?

Yes No   Do I tend to tease or "get back" at my teen by the things I say or the way I say them?

Yes No   Do I tend to be dogmatic or argumentative?

Yes No   Does my teen say that I think that I am always right?

Yes No   Does my teen say the tone of my voice sounds harsh or disapproving?

Yes No   Do I find myself not knowing or understanding what my teen has just said?

It is not easy for us to see ourselves clearly, to admit our mistakes, but honest self-examination may help us see what our teens see, and do something about it. Reflect on the questions answered *Yes*. Think about other ways you may kill conversation with your teen. When we can identify our problem, we provide ourselves a target at which to aim to improve our communicating skills.

4. CONTROLLING OUR EMOTIONS

We all overreact at times, and that is not all bad. While it is possible to pull something positive out of occasional eruptions of feelings, most of us likely would agree on the basis of experience that to maintain healthy communication with our teens, we need to control how we express our emotions.

Developing self-control is especially difficult when our teens lose control and take their frustrations out on us, but here are some strategies that work for most parents.

• Call "time out" when emotions get hot. When we notice that tempers are about to flare, we can say, "Let's take a break and talk more after dinner."

• Accept responsibility for our behavior. A human tendency is to blame others. We may see this most clearly in our children when they try to pin the blame for what they have done on others. If we don't accept responsibility for our actions, neither will our children.

• Respond to frustrating behavior in our teens with healthy action *before* we lose control. "I am unhappy to see you watching TV when you have so much homework to do. You need to turn it off until your work is done." As we see in the diagram, the longer we wait, the harder it is to respond objectively.

Neither the uncontrolled release of feelings nor their long-term suppression is healthy action. Talking calmly and firmly about what behavior we expect is the healthy approach. It's looking with our teens at the cause of the problem and attempting to deal with it together.

• Choose wisely what you will battle for. Many things just are not worth fighting about. In *Parenting Isn't for Cowards,* psychologist James Dobson tells the story of a woman who told him she had a very strong-willed twelve-year-old daughter. The mother said, "We have fought tooth and nail for this entire year. It has been awful! We argue nearly every night, and most of our fights are over the same issues." When Dr. Dobson asked her the cause of the conflict, she replied, "My daughter is

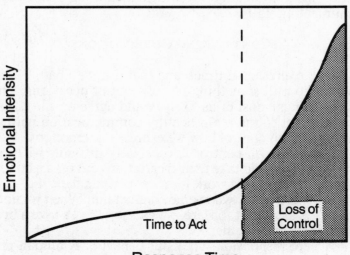

still a little girl, but she wants to shave her legs. I feel she's too young to be doing that and she becomes so angry that she won't even talk to me. This has been the worst year of our lives together!" Dr. Dobson looked at the mother and exclaimed, "Lady, buy your daughter a razor!"[4]

• Realize that our ability to respond to the demands of parenting is strongest when we have proper rest. A common cause of communication problems is fatigue. We simply are not at our best when we are tired. If a problem comes up when we are exhausted, a brief nap can enhance our ability to listen and talk effectively. On this point my son commented, "It's better to rest for twenty minutes and discuss a matter for ten minutes than to argue for thirty."

• Use "I" messages instead of "you" messages because "I" messages diminish defensive reactions and motivate positive responses.

"I" Messages	*"You" Messages*
—I feel frustrated when you don't do what I ask you to do.	—You never do what I ask you to do!
—I am angry, son. This is the third time my tools have been left outside.	—You make me so angry! You never remember to take my tools inside!

"I" messages help us release our feelings in ways that do not condemn our teens and destroy relationships.

If we find that we are unable to control our emotions, we need to seek professional help. We could be abusing our children verbally, if not physically. It is not a sign of weakness to get help from a pastor or qualified counselor; it is a sign of strength. Those who are weak will refuse to admit that they have a problem. They will attempt to ignore it, cover it up, or blame others. Often just talking about the problem with someone who will listen skillfully can relieve some of the burden. Talking it out can help us put the pieces of our lives together, gain a new perspective, and move forward.

5. Investing Time with Our Teens

According to one study, men were spending twice as much time with their children in 1980 as they did in 1960, but that merely means that they had increased their time from six to twelve minutes per day—*twelve* minutes to establish understanding, to really listen, to transfer significant values!

It takes time to communicate well. If we don't make the time, we don't listen. If we don't listen, we don't convey the acceptance teens need. If we don't convey acceptance, we don't help them build self-esteem and we don't win the right to be heard.

Some years ago, the song, "Cat's in the Cradle," convinced me of my need to invest quality time into the memory bank of my children.

> My child arrived just the other day;
> he came to the world in the usual way.
> But there were planes to catch and bills to pay;
> he learned to walk while I was away.
> And he was talkin' 'fore I knew it,
> and as he grew he'd say,
> "I'm gonna be like you, Dad,
> you know I'm gonna be like you.
> Chorus:
> And the cat's in the cradle and the silver spoon,
> little boy blue and the man in the moon.
> "When you comin' home, Dad?"
> "I don't know when, but we'll get together then;
> you know we'll have a good time then."
> My son turned ten just the other day;
> he said, "Thanks for the ball, Dad, come on
> let's play. Can you teach me to throw?"
> I said, "Not today, I got a lot to do."
> He said, "That's okay." And he,
> he walked away, but his smile
> never dimmed, it said, "I'm gonna be
> like him, yeah, you know I'm gonna be like him."

Chorus:
> Well he came from college just the other day;
> so much like a man I just had to say,
> "Son, I'm proud of you, can you sit for awhile?"
> He shook his head and he said with a smile,
> "What I'd really like, Dad, is to borrow the car keys;
> see you later, can I have them please?"

Chorus:
> I've long since retired, my son's moved away;
> I called him up just the other day.
> I said, "I'd like to see you if you don't mind."
> He said, "I'd love to, Dad, if I can find the time.
> You see, my new job's a hassle and the kids
> have the flu, but it's sure nice
> talkin' to you, Dad, it's been sure nice
> talking to you."
> And as I hung up the phone, it occurred to me,
> he'd grown up just like me;
> my boy was just like me.[5]

Powerful song. It makes me stop and reschedule my priorities.

How will we find the time in our busy schedules? The answer, of course, is that we won't "find" the time; we need to *create* it. Here are a few strategies that work:

• Control the TV before it controls you. The A.C. Nielson Company announced that the average American television set is on for forty-three hours, fifty-two minutes a week. That's more than *six hours a day.* Dolores Curran in her excellent book, *Traits of a Healthy Family,* writes: "Whether the breakdown in family communication leads people to excessive viewing or whether excessive television breaks into family lives so pervasively as to literally steal it from them, we don't know. . . . But we do know that we can become out of reach to one another when we're in front of a TV set."[6]

• Prioritize our activity schedule. In our fast-paced living, it is possible to have our time eaten away by activities that "demand" our time, but are not really significant to us. It may be helpful to list our activities on paper, including time spent with our teens, and organize them according to their

importance to us. Then we can schedule time with our teens
. . . hunting, fishing, shopping, going out to lunch, or just
talking. I find my teen is usually ready to talk at night. All I
need to do is to help get a snack, pull up a chair, and talk and
listen like a friend.

• Make the most of mealtime conversation. According to
Dr. Lee Salk, Cornell University's popular child psychologist,
many people neglect to do this. He writes: "People used to talk
and listen at meal time, but now they sit in front of their
television sets with their dinner. I don't care how busy you
are—you can take that time with your children."[7] Instead of
watching TV during mealtimes, we can ask questions about
our teens' day at school or work, avoiding complaints about
study habits or criticisms of friends. In Proverbs 17:1 we read,
"Better a dry crust with peace and quiet than a house full of
feasting, with strife." Before we speak it is well to ask ourselves, "Will discussion of this matter generate healthy discussion and strengthen family relationships?"

* * * * *

In summary, if we want healthy communication with our
teens, we will fight the common, everyday communication
barriers that can keep us from getting through. We will not
always win, but when we fail, we can adjust and try again to:

1. Win the right to be heard.
2. Develop a clear purpose of what we want to achieve in
   our communication with our teens.
3. Avoid conversation killers.
4. Control our emotions.
5. Invest time with our teens.

ACTION STEPS FOR POSITIVE COMMUNICATION

1. In order to better understand and relate to the attitudes and interests of your teen, ask yourself these four questions from the section, "Winning the Right to Be Heard." Jot
down your answers and let them guide your conversations.

— What activities/experiences is my teen involved in?
— How does my teen feel about these involvements?
— How can I best draw out my teen's thoughts and feelings?
— What concerns do we really need to talk about?

2. Building on the examples in the section, "Developing a Clear Purpose," write out your own purpose or goals for the kind of communication you want with your teen. Be specific.

3. If you haven't already done so, go back to the section, "Avoiding Conversation Killers," and answer the questions. Note the areas you need to work on. Write down what you can do today, this week.

4. Consider the strategies suggested in "Controlling Our Emotions" and develop a plan for implementing one or two that you think would be especially helpful for you.

5. From the ideas you gained in "Investing Time with Our Teens," write down some topics you could discuss at mealtime that would be of interest to your teen. It might be the school's football team, something you read in the newspaper, or how you feel about what happened to you at work. Think about how you can make the conversation fun so that your teen will want to come back for more.

Everyone should be quick to listen, slow
to speak . . . .

James 1:19

How to Listen So Teens Will Talk

The biggest mistake parents make is that they do not listen to
your whole argument. They always have an answer before
you're done.

Carl, 14

An Irish proverb states, "God gave us two ears and one
mouth, so we ought to listen twice as much as we speak." Our
teenagers' greatest need is for parents to listen to them, not as
children, but as human beings. Teenagers need to tell parents
their doubts, their dreams, and their bewilderment as they try
to discover why they were born, how they must live, and where
their future lies.

At first thought, the whole process of listening seems
rather simple. It is, after all, the part of communication that we
learn first and use most. (Listening takes 45% of our communication time on the average, speaking 30%, reading 16%, and
writing 9%.)[1] Yet we don't listen very well. We catch ourselves
saying, "How's that again?" "What did you say your name is?"
"Did you say I should turn right or left?"

One listening study reveals that after one ten-minute oral report, the average listener has heard, understood, and retained half of what was said. Within 48 hours, retention drops off another 50%, yielding a final comprehension of 25%. *Fortunately, listening is a skill we can improve.*

HOW DO YOU RATE AS A LISTENER?

Here is a listening inventory that will give you a rough estimate of how well you listen and will highlight areas in which improvement might be welcomed . . . by you and your teen.

1. On a scale of 1 (poor) to 5 (excellent), how would you rate yourself as a listener? _____
2. Using the same scale, how do you think the following people would rate you?

   Your Boss   _____
   Friends   _____
   Your Spouse   _____
   Your Teenager   _____

3. On a scale of 1 (low frequency) to 5 (high frequency), rate yourself on the *frequency* of the following good listening habits by circling the appropriate number.

   Low High
   1 2 3 4 5   I maintain direct eye contact.
   1 2 3 4 5   I focus my attention on what my teen is saying rather than what I am going to say next.
   1 2 3 4 5   I listen for feelings as well as facts.
   1 2 3 4 5   I avoid letting my mind wander.
   1 2 3 4 5   I tune in instead of tune out on difficult or controversial issues.
   1 2 3 4 5   I think first, then respond.
   1 2 3 4 5   I think of questions to ask and ask them.

To find your score for this quiz, add each of the numbers you circled. Then check your total points with the following:

32–35 Excellent
28–31 Good
13–27 Fair
7–12 Poor

* * * * *

Most of us rate ourselves far below our potential for effective listening, which means we realize the need for improvement. That awareness is the first step toward increasing listening skills. In this chapter we will discover *why* we don't listen as well as we could. We will focus on *how* to make the slight adjustments that produce significant improvements.

"MY TEEN WON'T TALK TO ME!"

A parent in Florida wrote, "Our daughter used to talk to us. She would tell us about her life—her friends, her school, everything that was of concern to her. About her 15th birthday, she just stopped talking."

Sometimes teens will talk for hours to their friends, but hardly at all to their parents. The disparity hurts. We may begin to resent our teens' friends, complain that our teens care more about their friends than they do us, and in various ways try to force them to notice us and pay attention to us. Of course this only makes matters worse.

Teens do not always know how to make sense of what they are thinking and feeling. Sometimes they fear that if they try to express themselves, it will come out all wrong. They are overly sensitive to being criticized or laughed at. Their *not talking* then becomes a defensive pattern designed to avoid confrontation and embarrassment.

We may be part of the problem. From our survey of over 800 teenagers, I compiled a list of their common complaints. According to them, we commonly

— jump to conclusions
— get angry when they don't immediately comply with our wishes
— interrupt

— give the impression we are too busy to be bothered
— talk too long without giving them a chance to speak
— become preoccupied with our own thoughts and feelings
— never ask questions
— never seem to want to know what they think
— don't understand how they feel.

One teen summarized the thoughts of others: "If my parents would only stop talking and listen to me for a change, we would get along much better." Another said, "Parents are human and understand everything because they have been through it all. But parents are not all the time great listeners."

You may find it interesting to ask your teen to be very candid and rate you on these complaints by putting a check in front of the ones that apply to you. Try not to be defensive or contradict what your teen says. Just listen. Ask questions to clarify. Perhaps this exercise could begin a new effort to understand yourself and your teen. You may not pull it off perfectly or immediately, because listening well takes practice and time. Be patient with yourself. One of the values of this exercise is that your teenager will know that you are interested and trying to build a better relationship.

LISTENING VS. HEARING

One teen said: "My parents hear me; my friends listen to me." Another young person, quoted in the *Christian Science Monitor,* said: "My parents say they want me to come to them with problems, but when I do they're busy or they only half listen and keep on doing what they were doing—like shaving or making a grocery list. If a friend of theirs came over to talk, they'd stop, be polite, and listen.[2]

These comments point to an important difference between hearing and listening. *Hearing* is a physical and mental process for the purpose of getting information. The focus is on what's happening inside the hearer's mind. Hearing constitutes only half-listening. *Listening* is not only a physical and mental process, it's also a psychological process. It operates at a deeper level and is designed to help one understand the person talking.

The focus is on what the one talking is thinking and feeling. Listening requires empathy, a psychological capacity to put one's self into the situation of the other. This calls for full attention.

When we listen well, we don't concentrate on what we are going to say next or criticize what is said or how it is said. We don't let our teens' tone of voice or appearance block out what they are saying. Instead of merely reacting, which is mindless, we respond, which is mindful.

Listening is the ability to hear another person so well that we are able not only to repeat what the person said, but also the feeling behind what was said . . . *to that person's satisfaction.* Can you remember how good it felt when someone listened to you that way? Imagine how effective listening would benefit your relationship with your teenager. Such listening almost always

— conveys genuine interest in what is being said
— avoids making wrong assumptions
— abstains from making judgmental statements
— helps our teens clarify their own thinking
— leads to solving problems
— builds self-esteem
— enhances the relationship
— increases mutual understanding.

ACE LISTENING SKILLS

Since listening, in contrast to hearing, can become a complex process, we are helped if we can follow a model or simple guide for increasing our skills. Here, then, is what I call the ACE Model for achieving expertise in listening: *A*ttending, *C*larifying, *E*valuating.

First, *attending* (paying attention) is making sure we are getting the message our teens are communicating. That message includes body signals (facial expression, gestures) and voice signals (tone, volume, inflection), as well as the words spoken. To sense the message correctly, we need to:

— calmly look in the eyes of our teens (but don't stare)
— hear the actual words being said

— pay attention to body signals, such as sad eyes, nervous hands, and tense lips
— eliminate distractions whenever possible (e.g., turn down the volume on the TV or shut a door)
— listen to the tone of voice.

Second, *clarifying* gets at the meaning of the message. It is normal for us to interpret messages according to *our* experience, *our* mental frame of reference, but it is detrimental since our experiences are likely to be vastly different from that of our teens. This may result in a limited match of meanings or no match at all. To me, homework includes studying for a test. But when I asked Jud, "Do you have any homework?", he said "No" even though he had three tests the next day because, to Jud, studying for a test is not the same as homework that is assigned.

To clarify whether our teens mean what we think their messages mean, we can paraphrase what we hear them say ("So what you're saying is _____. Right?"). Here are some additional clarifying responses:

— Can you give me an example of what you mean?
— How do you feel about what happened?
— What do you mean by _____? How would you define that word?
— If you take this action, what might be the consequences?
— Is this idea consistent with what you said before?
— What is the purpose of this activity?
— On a scale of 1 (least) to 10 (most), how important is this to you?
— What is your reason for saying (or doing) this?
— Do you think this is the right thing to do?
— What else can you tell me about this that will help me understand?

The beauty of sincerely asking questions like these is that we not only increase our understanding, but we also help our teens to clarify their own messages, hear their implications, and perhaps come to a wiser conclusion.

Third, *evaluating* is the stage where we mentally reflect

on the information we have gathered and decide how we will respond. Here it is important to consider our several options. For example:

— asking for more information
— remaining silent
— expressing our feelings
— stating our opinions
— choosing our words
— selecting our tone of voice.

We need to ask ourselves, "Which of the several options I have for responding to my teen will produce honest and the most effective communication?"

The ACE Model for listening effectiveness may seem to require a great deal of time to work through, but with a little practice, it saves time by increasing understanding.

APPLYING THE ACE MODEL

ACE skills generate positive responses by encouraging our teens to talk to us further.

Negative Responses	Positive Responses
—Did you fail your test again today?	—How did things go today at school?
—You think that's bad? When I was young . . .	—Tell me about it.
—You're out of your mind.	—That's a new idea.
—You're just getting yourself worked up.	—This seems important to you.
—You'll get over it.	—You must have felt frustrated.
—I've heard enough.	—I'd like to hear more.

Suppose your thirteen-year-old daughter comes to you and announces, "Dad, I've decided to go steady with Freddie." Some messages may go in one ear and out the other, but not this one. You're disturbed. The message has no rhyme or reason as far as you're concerned because your daughter is far too young to go "steady" the way you understand the word. You decide to apply the ACE Model for listening. In the following example, notice how the responses you make influence how your teen responds. Read through the negative responses first.

Teen: *Dad, I've decided to go steady with Freddie.*

Negative Responses	Positive Responses
You: You're too young to go steady!	You: Go steady?
Teen: No I'm not! All my friends are going steady.	Teen: Yes.
You: I don't care about your friends!	You: What does it mean to you to go steady?
Teen: You don't care about my friends? How could you say such a terrible thing?	Teen: Oh, you know, just being friends until another friend comes along.
You: I mean what your friends do is their business. You're not going steady!	You: When I was young, the term "going steady" was what you did just before you become engaged.
Teen: Well, if what my friends do is their business, then what I do is my business! You can't do anything about it!	Teen: Well, it doesn't mean that now. It would be stupid even to think about getting engaged.
You: Oh yes I can! You are grounded for the next two weeks!	You: I agree with that. Tell me more about this lucky guy Freddie.

At best, this is how the ACE Model for listening works. Can you sense its value? Imagine how it helps to avoid serious misunderstanding. And it really is not difficult. Once we get the basics fixed in our minds, we will find that the whole thinking process needed to apply the ACE Model can happen in a second or two. The model is built on the attitude that our teens are worth the effort necessary to get to know them, that their feelings and experiences are important to us, that we care about their well-being.

QUALITIES OF EFFECTIVE LISTENERS

Behind any strategy for good listening is the listener. In other words, who we are as persons is more important than any technique, however useful it might be. If we want to listen to our teens in such a way that our teens will talk to us, we will need to demonstrate the following qualities.

• *Desire.* Effective listeners want to listen. Most parents do not want to hear hassle, argument, impudence, or noise—the common opponents that block our best shots at listening effectively. When I face them, my preference is to give up and blame my son for the communication breakdown, but desire to listen keeps me going. Desire causes me to keep trying to get around the opponent: "Jud, I find it hard to listen when you argue with everything I say. I want to listen to what you are saying, but you need to hear me too."

• *Timing.* Effective listeners know when to listen. Sometimes that means knowing when the listening task is over. One night as I was working on this manuscript, Jud came bounding downstairs and said: "Dad, I'm reading a book that could have a profound influence on the course of my life . . . . It's kind of scary." I was so glad that my son wanted to share this big moment in his life with me that I stopped everything, asked some questions, and waited for him to expand on his thinking. But there wasn't anymore to be said right then. I think he felt he had been heard and his mind raced to a different task. I had to wait until later for extended listening.

• *Empathy.* Effective listeners can listen with the heart. Empathy is putting ourselves in the situation of our teens and understanding what they are feeling. Empathy requires

---

Teen: I'm not sure I want to go to college. I'm not sure that I can compete.

Reacting	*Responding*
Parent: Of course you can compete! Why do you think we spend all that money on private schools? You're no dummy.	Parent: I can understand that. I felt that way too before I went to college. After I got there, I found most of the students were a lot like me.

thinking first and then responding instead of reacting. Reacting is saying the first thing that comes to mind. Responding considers how what we say will affect our teens.

• *Self-Control.* Effective listeners remember that feelings come and go, that what is said by a teen in a fit of anger probably is not a true representation of the teen's real thoughts and feelings. One mother told me that her teen yelled at her, "I hate you!" The mother felt like crying and yelling back something about her daughter's ingratitude. Instead, she chose to stay in control of herself and the situation. She said, "Sue, I realize you are very angry at me right now, but it's not OK for you to say that you hate me. I want you to know that when you are ready to talk, I will be ready to listen. Even though I may not agree with you, I care very much about you and how you feel." Keeping the channels of communication open is the best way to achieve reconciliation. It's not easy, especially when our teens' language or actions seem calculated to make us angry, hurt, or upset. It requires a commitment to keep our emotions in check.

• *Skill.* Effective listeners make the ACE Model for listening a habit. They are fun to talk to, a delight to be around. Even if they are not brilliantly articulate, they know how to bring out the best in the one talking to them. I like the way someone once described this kind of listening ace:

> His thoughts were slow,
> His words were few, and never formed to glisten.
> But he was a joy to all his friends—
> You should have heard him listen.

WHEN TEENS STILL WON'T TALK

It may be that reading this chapter has made you feel guilty for not listening better. When you compare your performance to the qualities and techniques suggested here, perhaps you realize you don't measure up very well. The truth is that none of us is perfect. We all can improve.

Admitting our mistakes not only to ourselves, but also to our teens can break down listening barriers. For example, we can say to our teens: "In the past I have tuned you out. I'm really sorry. Will you forgive me? I want to do much better. If there are times when you feel that I'm not listening, please let me know. I won't hold what you say against you. I really want to know." But parents can do only so much. Teens must take responsibility too.

Suppose after trying all this your teen still doesn't talk to you. Teenagers seem to go through a stage when the answer to every question is a grunt. During this time, nothing seems to work. Even an expert communicator can't get them to talk. It's well to keep in mind that this stage is likely as unhappy and frustrating a time for our teens as it is for us. Usually it's intermittent and doesn't last.

If we have taken the steps toward effective listening recommended in this chapter and we get no response, we must not give up. If we persevere, our teens will not only talk to us, but will want to learn to listen as well. Perhaps we will one day hear the kind of response a sixteen-year-old in Florida wrote to us,

The one message I want to tell my mother is that I love her and that I'm here too if she needs to talk to someone.

ACTION STEPS FOR POSITIVE COMMUNICATION

1. Review the first section of this chapter in which you rated yourself as a listener. Check or star the areas you want to improve and complete this sentence: In order to improve my ability to listen, I will _____.

2. After reading the section on why teens don't talk, reflect on the reasons your teen may be reluctant to talk. Then fill in this chart according to your honest assessment of the problem. You will be taking a giant step toward the solution.

Reasons for Not Talking	*Strategies Worth Trying*
a.	a.
b.	b.
c.	c.

3. Which of the three ACE listening skills (Attending, Clarifying, Evaluating) do you feel you need to strengthen? For example, do you pay attention to the full message (facial, tonal,

verbal) of your teen? _____ Do you ask clarifying questions to gain understanding? _____ Do you evaluate how your responses will affect the quality of the communication? _____ What will you do this week to strengthen that skill?

4. How would you respond if your teen said, "I don't think I'll ever get married!'"? In the space below, try writing positive responses that reflect your desire to listen and then write what you think your teen's response to you might be. I'll fill in the dialogue for the negative responses.

I don't think I'll ever get married!

Negative Responses	*Positive Responses*
Parent: That's ridiculous!	Parent:
Teen: No it's not! A lot of people never get married!	Teen:
Parent: You're too young to know what you think!	Parent:

5. Which qualities of effective listeners listed in this chapter are most characteristic of you? _____ Which qualities do you want to strengthen? _____ Drawing upon the information in this chapter and your own experience, what will you do this week to strengthen this quality? _____

We start talking to each other, but we
finish screaming at each other. Then I
don't talk to them for about a week.

John, 15

How Communication
Works and What to
Do When It Doesn't

Most of us know as much about communication as we
know about the engines of our cars—which isn't very much.
We get in our cars, turn on the motors, and simply drive. We
don't worry about *how* the motor works . . . until it breaks
down and leaves us stranded.

Communication with our teens is sometimes like that. We
don't think about how it works until something goes wrong. If
we knew what went wrong and why, we could more effectively
repair the problem.

Good communication takes more effort than we might
expect. Perhaps because most of us think that communicating is easier than it really is we tend to become discouraged
when we run into difficulty. Although effort is needed, the
mechanics are not really difficult to learn. Sometimes only
slight adjustments will solve the problem. With the right
tools, clear directions, and time to get it straight, we can make
the repairs.

WHAT IS COMMUNICATION?

Communication is . . .

a laugh
a handshake
a tear
a frown
a gesture
a word
a kiss
a tone
a smile
a whisper
a scream
a wink
a pause
a grunt
a hug.

"Communication" comes from a Latin word which means "to make common, to share." It refers to the process of transferring a message or meaning from one person's mind to the mind of another through such means as words, body signals, tone of voice. Actually, *no real communication takes place until the other person interprets the message the way the transmitting person intends it to be understood.* Only then is there a common meaning, a shared message, a meeting of the minds.

On the surface, this process seems as simple as driving a car, a matter of habit, but if we look under the "hood" we see seven distinct parts that make the whole process work—or fail. When we talk to someone, all these parts are in "motion" and dynamically affecting each other, as do the parts of a running engine. It can get pretty complex. Let's simplify the process by looking at each part of the communication process.

First, we need a *sender* of a message. As senders, we play the most important part in communicating with our teens. Centuries ago, Aristotle discovered that the *ethos* or personal qualities of the one sending a message were most critical to the success of that message. These qualities include patience,

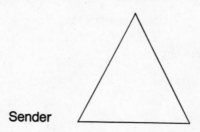

openness, empathy, honesty, integrity, and love. Nothing in communications research today contradicts that finding.

To improve communication skills with our teens, we need to realize that success in getting through to them depends primarily on us. We need to take responsibility for initiating changes in areas such as patience, openness, and empathy to increase our effectiveness.

Next in the communication process is *coding,* which means formulating the ideas.

From numerous options available to us, we mentally select certain ideas to express and the particular words, tone of voice, and facial expression which will make up our message. All of this happens very fast and is usually a matter of mental habit.

What results is the *message.*

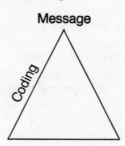

The message is what we transmit to our teens. It's what they see, feel, and hear.

Then comes the process of *decoding* or interpreting the message by the one receiving it.

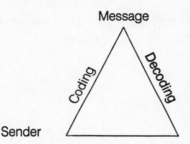

Here our teens add their interpretation to what we have said. What it means to them may or may not be what we intended.

The *receiver* is the one who decodes or tries to understand the message.

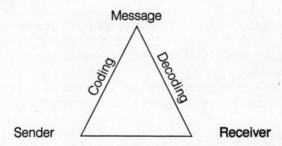

As receivers, our teens' disposition, attitudes, and habits of thinking influence the way they interpret our messages.

That's not all. Another factor is *relationship.* Although

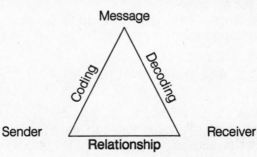

a part of that relationship, perhaps a large part, will remain constant, and is not easily changed, some part will change in each encounter (one moment a teen may be happy, the next sad), giving a fresh dynamic to the communication process.

Adding even greater complexity to the process is the *context* in which our communications occur.

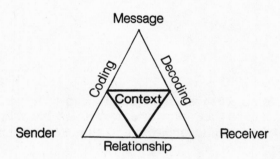

Context includes the time, place, and circumstances such as the presence of friends or the pressure of a final exam. The context also directly affects what is said, how it is said, and what is heard.

When we combine these parts, we see how the seven-fold process of transferring meaning fits together:

1. The sender
2. formulates an idea
3. into a transmitted message
4. interpreted
5. by the receiver
6. in reference to his relationship to the sender
7. within a particular context.

A SEVEN-STEP REPAIR MANUAL

At times I have wished that I had said something differently or not at all. Perhaps you too have had to explain: "I didn't mean that the way it sounded." "What did I say to cause you to think that?" "That wasn't what I really meant." Such misunderstanding is common in most homes, as a Chinese proverb reminds us:

> Nobody's family can hang out the sign,
> "Nothing the matter here."

A ninth-grader wrote in one of our surveys: "Some parents don't talk to their children because they're so afraid that if they say something wrong then everything will fall apart." Communication usually falls apart when our messages are not understood the way we intended. Knowing which of the seven parts of the communication process to repair is the first step in making the process workable.

1. The Sender

Several years ago, Marshall McLuhan stated that "the *medium* is the message." He meant that the way we say a message is more important than the words themselves. Thus when there is a problem in talking with our teens, the first trouble spot to check is ourselves.

Transactional analysis (TA) provides a useful tool for analyzing ourselves and the way we come through to our teens. In TA theory, persons exhibit three types of expression or "ego states," *regardless of their age,* which are labeled as Parent, Adult, and Child (P, A, C).[1] Most conversations follow one of the following three patterns:

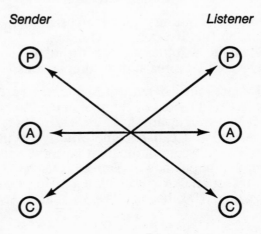

Note that the way a sender expresses his personality (as P, A, or C) influences the way the receiver responds.

Parent expressions tend to raise the status of the sender and belittle the status of the listener. These expressions are characterized by:

> scolding, condemning, yelling, lecturing,
> commanding, ordering, warning, criticizing,
> advising, put-downs, inattentiveness, anger,
> insensitivity, a harsh tone of voice.

They influence the listener to respond in a Child pattern and are counterproductive to good communication.

Adult expressions are honest and nondefensive. They draw out the best in listeners and treat them as persons of equal worth, as when a father sits down with his teenage son for a "man-to-man" talk. Adult expressions are characterized by:

> mutuality, respect, openness,
> sensitivity, directness, a readiness
> to listen, honest expression of feelings.

This ego state encourages the listener to reciprocate with Adult expressions.

Child expressions in TA theory are sometimes spontaneous, lively, and fun-loving, except when we don't get our way. All of us act childish at times. In the Child mode we want to be served, coddled, the center of attention, free of responsibility. The Child ego state is further characterized by:

> emotional outbursts, anger, frustration,
> irresponsibility, talking too much,
> dogmatic attitudes, unclear meanings,
> revengeful desires, unfair comparisons.

This style influences the listener to respond in a Parent mode.

Parent and Child modes of expression tend to block communication. If I am not aware that I am taking part in Parent or Child transactions, I can become bitterly entangled in a network of unpleasant communication patterns and not have the foggiest notion about how to get out. On the other hand, I can use Transactional Analysis as a tool to analyze what pattern I'm using. If I become aware that I am sending

Parent-style messages, I can change to Adult messages and elicit a more Adult response.

Strategies

• Analyze yourself. In conversations that seem to be ineffective, ask yourself: "Am I expressing myself like a Parent, Child, or Adult? How do I want to come across? What do I need to do to change?"

• Act in the present. Recognize that there may be a connection between the way we tend to express ourselves in the present (as P, A, or C) and all of our past emotional experiences and behavioral habits. In fact, a feeling of "I'm not OK" might be caused by the past, not the present. Decide to act in the present against such inhibiting and crippling feelings of the past. The change we want will likely not come all at once, but by choosing the ego state that we want to express, we will have begun to move out of the tyranny of the past and exercise self-direction in the present.

• Put the Adult you in charge. Avoid using Parent words like *should, always, never, stupid, grow up* or Child vocabulary punctuated by *I want, I need, I wish, I won't, I can't.* Use Adult expressions that convey openness, flexibility, positive assertiveness, and sensitivity to our teen's point of view. For example, *What do you think? We might . . . , Let's try to . . . , It seems best to . . . , What if . . . .*

• Draw out our teens' best qualities. Concentrate on enabling our teens to shift from a Child or Parent mode to an Adult mode by maintaining our own Adult ego state even when our teens are acting obnoxiously. Don't repay bad talk with bad talk. Keep in mind that what we give will eventually be very similar to what we get.

2. The Coding Process

When we formulate an idea into words, we often lack clarity. We know what we mean, but the way we formulate that meaning makes it hard for our teens to understand. We lack clarity for three reasons.

First, we assume that our words have only one meaning—

the one *we* give them. Actually, our words have an almost unlimited variety of possible meanings so it is understandable if our teens misunderstand. The 500 most common words in the English language have a combined total of 14,070 meanings—an average of more than twenty-eight per word. We may intend the simple message "I want you home at a reasonable hour" to mean before 11:00 P.M. while our teens may interpret "reasonable" to mean 1:00 A.M.

Second, we may not articulate every detail that we have in mind because we *assume* the connections are self-evident. However, our teens may miss the implied details altogether.

What I said	*What I meant*
Jud, please mow the grass.	Jud, please mow the grass *this morning* because it looks like it is going to rain this afternoon.

Unless I say what I mean, Jud is left to fill in the thought. Any normal teenager is going to complete the thought this way: "Please mow the grass *sometime.*"

Third, we may be unclear because we intend to be indirect. Indirectness can be a game in which we hint at what we mean and challenge others to fill in the blanks. The upside of the game is that indirect communication can create a sense of rapport, of being on the inside of meaning that nonfamily members would not understand. The downside is that family members likely will be left in a fog, too.

Sometimes parents are indirect because there is a "pay-off." It provides the parent with a defense or way out of a difficult situation. If a statement backfires, the parent can always claim, "I didn't mean that!" However, such indirectness prolongs *misunderstanding* and develops a communication pattern that is basically dishonest, weak, and counterproductive.

To correct coding errors, ask yourself these questions:

— What do I really want to say?
— What words and facial expressions will convey that meaning?
— Am I making any unwarranted assumptions?

— Am I skipping any logical steps in conveying my idea?
— Am I being clear and direct?

3. *The Message*

How can we create messages that are well received by our teenagers? The answer is to pay attention not only to one's words, but also to tone of voice and facial expression. Our messages are tied very closely to the *way* we present them. Albert Mehrabian, a UCLA communications researcher, startled people with the results of his extensive research which showed that the spoken message impacts an audience in the following way:

— Word messages—what we say—account for 7% of what is believed.
— Tone of voice messages—the way we say it—account for 38%.
— Non-verbal messages—what is seen—account for an incredible 55% of what a listener will believe.[2]

The following diagram depicts the comparative impact of the verbal, tonal, and visual aspects of our messages.

Message Impact

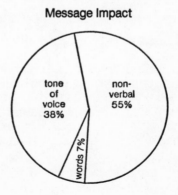

Each of these message areas can communicate a positive or negative impact. Check the following items that you honestly think are characteristic of your messages to your teen. Then, if you feel brave enough, ask your teen to check the items he or she thinks are typical of you.

Word Messages

Negative Words	*Positive Words*
____ Don't be ridiculous!	____ I like the way you . . . .
____ Are you crazy?	____ Tell me about it.
____ You always	____ I'd like to hear more.
____ You never	____ How can I help?
____ How many times must I tell you?	____ You must have felt really frustrated.
____ That's stupid!	____ I love you.

Tone of Voice Messages

Negative Tone		*Positive Tone*	
____ sarcastic	____ blaming	____ caring	____ satisfied
____ tense	____ angry	____ concerned	____ joyful
____ frustrated	____ blaring	____ affirming	____ cheerful
____ judgmental	____ hard	____ relaxed	____ supportive
____ rejecting	____ scared	____ tender	____ calm
____ emotional	____ harsh	____ loving	____ objective

Nonverbal Messages

Negative Signals		*Positive Signals*	
____ frowning	____ smirking	____ smile	____ eye contact
____ crying	____ disgust	____ touching	____ head nod
____ pointing	____ jabbing	____ open arms	____ relaxed body
____ rude gestures		____ attentive face	
____ throwing up hands		____ forward lean	
____ distance extension		____ distance reduction	

Strategies: To gain greater control over words, tone of voice, and the nonverbal aspects of messages, consider the following:

• Words: think before you speak. An extra second or two can give you time to select the words that will more accurately convey your message.

• Tone: listen to your own voice as if you were your teen. Ask whether your tone conveys the message you intend. Will it produce the effect you want?

• Non-verbal signals: check body and facial expressions in a mirror if possible. Ask, "Do I look relaxed, accepting, open to my teen's feelings?" If we do not look relaxed or open, we can simply tell ourselves, "Relax!" or "Be open!" It's amazing what a little self-talk can do to increase the consistency of our messages.

4. The Decoding Process

The process by which messages are interpreted is called decoding. When the decoding of messages is faulty, the intended message is misunderstood. If we are talking, the decoding process is really the responsibility of our teens, but there are some things we can do to help them decode accurately.

Strategies

• Think about the way you coded some message that caused an emotional outburst in your teen. What could you have done to increase the chances for an objective response?

• Analyze current disputes with your teen. Are the disputes caused by decoding errors? For example, if I ask Jud to mow the grass and he interprets that to mean *sometime* when I mean *now,* I have a communication breakdown caused by a decoding error. But it is my fault, not his. The decoding error is caused by my failure to code my message clearly enough. Such misunderstandings can generate prejudice on my part ("my son is lazy") and lead to reactions on my son's part ("my dad is unreasonable") that produce counterreactions in a vicious cycle—all unnecessary.

• Be alert to responses that suggest your teen is not interpreting you correctly. Ask, "Do you know what I mean?" or say, "I'm not sure I'm being clear on this point. Let me try again to say what I mean."

• Keep in mind that when our teens (or anyone, for that matter) fail to interpret what we say in the way we intend, they do not *intend* to misunderstand us. Thus we ought not make them feel guilty if they misunderstand us. So much can be lost as we try to formulate, communicate, and translate ideas that it really is a wonder we understand one another at all.

5. The Receiver

How teenagers feel from one day to the next will also influence how they receive our messages. One mother told me that her daughter can be ranting and raving one minute and calm and sweet the next. Maybe the problem is a chemical imbalance, such as hypoglycemia, or the inner turbulence and changes of adolescence.

Since teens are in the process of change, they often don't understand themselves. They say things they don't mean. They feel things they don't say. They are so preoccupied with figuring themselves out that often they don't listen very well. They can scream hatred to their parents and yet at the same time be fiercely loyal to them. They can think so highly of themselves and so little of themselves that at times not much of what we say will get through that fog. Unfortunately, we may see them so quickly mirror our worst traits and so seldom express our best, that we can be easily discouraged.

All is not hopeless. After all, we didn't turn out all that bad. And there are some things we can do that will help our teens to understand us.

Strategies

• Relax. Who our teens are now and how they listen to us is not necessarily indicative of how they will be when they reach our age. Time is on our side. Count on the long view of who your teen will become.

• Remember. Think about the preoccupations you had as a teen that sometimes screened out what your parents said. Then, be patient. Say the same message again to your teen if it's important, perhaps another way and another day.

• Reflect. If you were in the shoes of your teen, how would your messages be received? What changes in tone of voice, body signals, or choice of words could you make that would help your teen to listen to you?

6. The Relationship

When my son Jud returned home from an eleven-day choir concert tour through Tennessee, Virginia, and Washington, D.C., the choir performed for all the parents and friends of those in the choir. I thought the concert was superb, exciting, moving! The next week my family and I heard another choir of teenagers who were on tour. To me, the concert seemed unduly long and boring. The likely difference? Relationship.

Relationships influence perceptions. When relationships are good, we are more apt to be open, receptive, affirming. When they are not so good, we may come across as being more critical and less tolerant. Sometimes our relationships with our teens change as our moods change. One day the strength of the relationship could stand any attack. The next day it may seem to hang by a thread. We may feel very good about our teens while our teens may still be nursing some grudge or resentment based in the past.

Whatever the relationship, it is bound to influence our communication. Knowing this fact will cause us to examine our relationship as one of the seven key factors determining the success or failure of our communication.

Strategies

• Admit how you feel in order to help your teen understand you. Use "I" statements rather than "You" statements to decrease blame and defensiveness and to increase understanding. Notice the difference and imagine the effect of each on your teen.

"You" Statements	*"I" Statements*
—You make me frustrated. You haven't done what I asked you to do.	—I feel frustrated when things I asked you to do are left undone.
—You make me so mad that I don't want to talk to you!	—I feel too angry toward you right now to talk straight. Let's continue our conversation later.

• Let your teen know what you want the relationship to be like. This will lift attention off any feelings of rejection or anger and focus it on the long-range goal and character of the relationship. For example, you might say:

> We are having a difficult time accepting each other right now. But I want you to know that even though your behavior is driving me up the wall, deep down I accept you. I love you, I'll be happy when we can solve our problem.

7. The Context

Words effective in one situation can have negative results in another. I recently overheard an argument between a father and his teenager. The boy had just come home from mowing a lawn. He was hot, sweaty, and exhausted. The father was exasperated that his son had not done something asked of him. Neither was ready to be civil or listen to the other. The result was a nasty tirade of words that could not help but damage a relationship. Perhaps if the father had waited until both were more comfortable, the damage could have been prevented.

Part of the wisdom of King Solomon was his awareness of the importance of timing.

> There is a time for everything, and a season
> for every activity under heaven . . .
> a time to be silent and a time to speak . . . .[3]

Warning lights about the possibility of contextual problems should come on when we or our teens are:

— tired
— busy with a project
— studying or reading the paper
— trying to solve some problem
— watching TV
— in the presence of friends or other people
— not feeling well physically
— depressed or moody.

Strategies

• Watch for the warning lights mentioned above. If any of these conditions exist, you might say: "I need to discuss something with you, but I can see this is not a good time. When can we talk?"

• If your teen is experiencing one of the warning light conditions, it may provide an excellent opportunity to show *empathy* (e.g., "I sense you are very tired. Right?"). Ask yourself: "If I were in my teen's situation, how would I want my parent to respond to me?"

• You and your teen are likely coming from *different* contexts. Before you speak, you need to consider not only whether the time and place are right for you, but whether it is right also for your teen.

REACHING OUR DESTINATION

Repairing communication breakdowns with your teen may be too difficult for you to do alone. You may need the help of a certified clinical psychologist or a pastor, priest, or rabbi trained in family counseling. Additional reading from the recommended book list at the back of this book can be helpful as well as cassettes on parent-teen communication. Whatever it takes, do it.

You cannot force your teen to respond to you in certain ways, but you can do whatever is in your power by increasing your understanding of what communication is, working through the seven-step repair manual, and letting your teen know that you will go the extra mile to reach a mutually satisfying destination.

You might not reach your destination immediately. The son of a friend of mine couldn't stand his father's discipline. As soon as he was old enough, he escaped the discipline by joining the Marines! Six months later the son called his father and said, "Dad, there are several men in my group who can't take the pressure. They're falling like flies. The only reason I'm still here is that you taught me the value of discipline. Thank for hanging in there, Dad."

ACTION STEPS FOR POSITIVE COMMUNICATION

1. As you reflect on the TA diagram on page 69, which of the three possibilities do you think most often represents the kind of transactions you have with your teen? When the transactions are unsatisfying, determine what you will do to repair the problem.

2. When you formulate your message, think about what you can do to ensure that it is decoded accurately.

3. If your messages are not received the way you intend them, determine whether the primary problem is nonverbal signals, tone of voice, or the words themselves. If you're not sure of the answer, ask your spouse or a friend who will be honest with you about your voice tone, body or facial signals, and the words you tend to use when talking to your teen.

4. When you feel the relationship with your teen is strained, determine to make it stronger. Choose at least one thing you can start doing immediately to make it strong and take action on it.

5. If communication sometimes breaks down because of the wrong time and place, think of some creative ways to provide a context that generates freedom of expression (taking a walk, moving to another room of the house, going out for something to eat).

When my parents and I get mad at each other, there is yelling, "going wild," and slapping.

Jennifer, 14

Responding Calmly to Strong Emotions

Although statistics show an alarming increase in damaged relationships from both parent and child physical abuse, *verbal abuse* is likely even more prevalent and sometimes inflicts greater pain than physical blows. Who can count the damaged emotions and the broken relationships resulting from sledgehammer words and emotions that have gone wild? Between teenagers and their parents, verbal abuse occurs when feelings are not controlled and there is no plan for responding effectively to strong emotions.

In our communication survey, we asked 800 teenagers what happens when they and their parents become angry with each other. Here's a sample of their responses.

My mom will go over her list of my faults. Sometimes she yells and says she's not yelling.

John, 12

We just yell at each other. Then I run to my room, slam the door, and blast my radio.

Nancy, 12

I yell at them and try to win the argument. Usually I lose.

Jan, 15

When my mom and I argue, we usually just yell at each other and then go into our rooms. But eventually we make up because it affects me very much when the two of us just fight.

Guy, 16

My dad usually lectures me.

Tom, 13

Dad will start yelling at whoever gets in his way. Mom gets all mushy about everything.

Ginger, 13

There is some yelling, some talking back, and a lot of walking away.

Robert, 13

I get yelled at and then I get in trouble for yelling.

Cindy, 15

My mom kind of gets tired and stares. My dad raises his voice and sighs.

Robin, 13

As parents we are not well-trained to respond to strong words and feelings. We are often baffled by the intensity and the unpredictability of our teen's emotional outbursts. Perhaps just as often, we are surprised at our own responses—our angry reactions and ineffective attempts to regain control.

It is not easy to respond effectively. To reduce the number and severity of communication breakdowns and to increase understanding, we need to use a clear plan we can remember. When strong feelings are present, parents and teens need to respond CALMLY, an acronymn suggesting a five-point plan.

C = CONTROL YOUR RESPONSES

We are a nation of shouters. When asked what happens when emotions get hot in the home, one seventh-grader quipped, "Let the yelling begin!" More than 70 percent of the teenagers in our survey complained that their parents yell at them. Some parents admit that in the heat of the moment their feelings get the best of them. They claim that usually there is a good reason for screaming ("It's his fault!" or "She made me mad!") and that "the words just come out." Is there some mysterious force that makes us say things in a way we can't control?

Freud and Darwin have all but convinced us there is something uncontrollable in us (the "id" and the primal "beast") that screams for release. So we have been taught to holler when we feel like it and "let it all hang out." It will make us feel better. It will clear the air. It will release pent-up emotional energy. It's good for us, they say.

I'm not convinced. While there are positive uses of anger and healthy, even loud, expressions of it, in all my counseling, I have never seen relationships between husband and wife or parents and children helped by yelling. Quite the contrary. Yelling, because it's rude, almost always ensures that no one listens. It attacks relationships, entrenches positions, provokes wrath, kills dialogue. I get angry at the simplistic notion that it's OK for parents to express anger any way they want without regard to what it does to the psyche of their teenagers. I get angry at the narcissism of a "me and my" generation that screams because it makes them feel better.

The problem is not with rip-roaring debate or argument. It's not wrong to strongly disagree or express deep feelings about a matter. The problem is when the expression of feeling is uncontrolled and disregards human relationships.

Suzy is still suffering from what her mother did in a fit of anger ten years earlier. She wrote: "When I was seven, my mother told me I was spoiled and horrible and that it was my fault that my dad left."

I believe we can control our emotions. Feelings are subject to thoughts and thoughts are subject to choice. In a highly acclaimed book entitled, *Anger,* social psychologist Carol Tavris writes, "Self-control, especially self-control in the pursuit of emotional restraint, is a human choice, beyond the limitations of instinct."[1]

Consider the father who is snarling mad at his son. The phone rings. A very important client wants to talk with the father. What happens to the father's tone of voice? His choice of words? His raging anger? They are immediately brought under control by choice.

When we notice feelings such as anger, frustration, hurt, insecurity, bitterness, envy, or revenge, we can and must choose our words carefully. When we think about what we really want to say and the emotional effect we want our words to have, we increase our options for constructive responses and we remain in control.

Emotional Statement

Sue: I am old enough to do what I want. Ted asked me to go to the movie with him and I'm going. I don't care what you say!

Negative Choice

You: No, you're not old enough to do what you want! Listen, smarty, I'm still the boss!

Sue: You can't stop me!

You: Oh yes I can!

Sue: How?

You: Sheer force if that is what it takes!

Sue: I'll climb out the window!

You: If you try it I'll make you wish you never had!

Sue: What would you do?

You: I won't let you back in!

Sue: That's really dumb! First you won't let me out, then you won't let me back in!

Positive Choice

You: Sue, you are old enough to make certain decisions, but I have strong feelings about your going out tonight.

Sue: Why?

You: Because you have a term paper due tomorrow and you wanted my help with one part of it.

Sue: Well, I can just show you what I want you to do and I can type it when I get home.

You: No, Sue. I will not work on it without you here. The term paper is your responsibility, not mine.

Sue: You're impossible? You don't care about my date!

You: I'm sorry it seems that way to you. I do care about you.

Notice that in the negative choice column, the conversation degenerates to threats, name-calling, and sarcasm. It is likely that in such an exchange, feelings would be hurt, the relationship jeopardized, and the argument unresolved. In the positive choice column, emotions are still high at the end, but no real damage has occurred. The parent has remained firm, expressed positive regard for the teen, and retained verbal self-control. Positive choices don't guarantee resolutions, but they allow expression without damage to the relationship.

A = AVOID VICIOUS CYCLES

When we have had "words" with our teens and tempers have flared, we are in a combat danger zone. Our tendency is to become defensive, guarded, and focused only on ourselves. Some parents attack verbally as a way of gaining the advantage or at least "getting even." Unfortunately, the bumper sticker message, "I don't get mad. I get even!" is often true of parents' relationships with their own children. At a parenting conference I attended, a mother announced unashamedly, "I want my daughter to know how badly I feel when she embarrasses me in public so I make a point of embarrassing her in front of her friends." If we want our relationships to be healthy and satisfying, we must avoid the vicious cycle of attack and counterattack.

Nancy, 15, describes what happens when she and her father argue.

> My dad gets mad easily. When he's mad he doesn't want to talk about it. I say, "Dad, I want to talk about it." And he says "No, not now." And I'll say, "But Dad, we have got to talk about it *now!*" Then I'll get mad and start screaming at him because he puts me off. That makes him more mad and he starts yelling at me. Finally I leave and go to my room. It always happens that way.

It doesn't always have to happen that way. Whatever our limitations, however much we have generated endless rounds of arguing in the past, we can avoid the cycle of verbal attack and counterattack.

Strategies

• Discover patterns. Get a mental grip on the argumentative pattern. Learn how it develops. Ask yourself: "Who usually initiates the attack and who keeps it going?" Try to describe the way it appears to you.

— My son contradicts what I say.
— Anger begins to build until finally I yell.
— Both of us experience hurt feelings.

— I lash out with threats; my son goes to his room and turns on his stereo. The problem surfaces again later.
— We don't talk to each other for days.

The cycle can be illustrated this way.

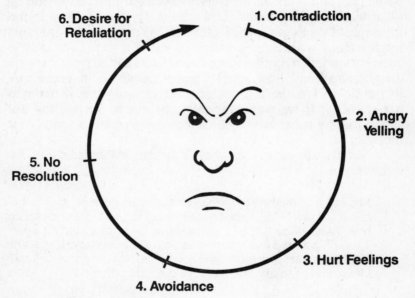

6. Desire for Retaliation

1. Contradiction

2. Angry Yelling

5. No Resolution

3. Hurt Feelings

4. Avoidance

• Break cycles. Any vicious cycle requires two or more people. If you know what the pattern is, you can break it by not responding as you usually would. You can't control how your teen will respond, but you do have a number of options about what to say that can break the cycle.

— Our words and tone of voice are not coming out right. How can we say what we are feeling in a better way?
— Both of us need time to cool off. Let's talk again at 4:00 P.M.
— I really do want to understand you, but right now I'm very frustrated. I need to work through my own feelings before I can listen to you the way I want to. Let's talk after supper.

— Jim, yelling is not acceptable. I know you are angry and maybe you have a right to be. But you don't like it when I yell at you. And I don't like it when you yell at me. Lower your volume and I promise I will hear you out.

Whatever you say to break the vicious cycle, you will need to take the initiative. That's hard, but not impossible. Taking the initiative involves a simple but firm choice to take positive action.

• Delay reaction. When you are not clear about how to proceed, give yourself time to think, time to control your emotions instead of letting them control you. Even a few seconds can enable you to choose words and a tone of voice that can stop the cycle rather than perpetuate it.

• Encourage expression. Not talking about feelings only increases tension. Encourage your teen to put his feelings into words. Talk about why the feelings are so strong. Try to focus attention not on who's to blame, but on how to solve the problem.

• Stay calm. Don't fight anger with anger. My own father and my son think this is the most important strategy. I agree. The writer of Proverbs provides several insights supporting the need for calmness.

— A gentle answer turns away wrath, but a harsh word stirs up anger.[2]

— A hot-tempered person stirs up dissension, but a patient person calms a quarrel.[3]

— A fool gives full vent to his anger, but a wise person keeps himself under control.[4]

— For as churning the milk produces butter, and as twisting the nose produces blood, so stirring up anger produces strife.[5]

L = LISTEN TO THE TEEN PERSPECTIVE

What seems to frustrate teens most are the times when they think their parents are not listening to them. In our survey, Jud and I asked teenagers, "In your opinion, what is the biggest mistake made by parents?"

Before listening and trying to understand, they yell and then things get worse.

Sam, 16

They don't listen to your whole argument. They always answer before you are done.

Brent, 14

Not giving me a chance to express my opinion.

Sharon, 14

Not listening to me. Not hearing me out first and then deciding calmly.

Susan, 14

Forgetting adolescent feelings and thoughts.

Eva, 15

Parents don't always let the teenager tell their half of the story. A lot of times they jump to conclusions.

Doug, 14

Some parents counter:

— We know what the facts are. Why waste more time?
— We've heard the same story a hundred times. We're sick of it.
— When my daughter gets all emotional, I just tune her out. She reminds me of my mother.
— When my son feels strongly about something, he gets so dogmatic and arrogant. It drives me up the wall.

Both parents and teens have points. Parents can be downright insensitive and teens can be completely unreasonable, but unless we fully hear each other's perspective on an issue, we may very well argue about something of no consequence or something we really do agree upon!

I have been impressed by a very simple illustration that is easily remembered and helps me whenever I too quickly assume I know what my son is thinking and feeling. Suppose someone were to take a tennis ball painted white on one side and black on the other, and hold it between my son and me. If asked, "What color is it?", I would answer with the color that I see.

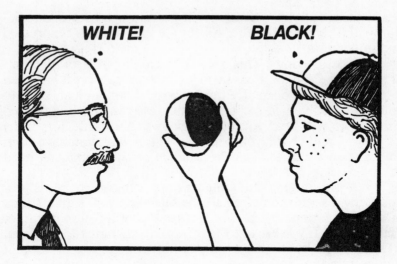

My son would answer with the opposite color. Neither of us would be able to agree, no matter how long we argued, until the ball was turned and we saw each other's perspective.

I have often wondered how many painful arguments could be avoided if only we made the effort to see how things look from the other's point of view. If we listen well enough to see our teens' perspective, the chances are great that they will reciprocate by listening to our point of view.

Strategies

• Accept responsibility. Since we are older, more mature, and *the parents,* we bear responsibility for doing our part to build quality and understanding into the relationship. We are not responsible for our teens' words, attitudes, or actions that we did not cause, but we are responsible for our choice of words, tone of voice, body language, and behavior.

• Understand feelings. Feelings are more important than facts. When emotions are high, focus your attention on understanding the feelings your teen is experiencing. Teens will not feel understood until they have adequately expressed how they feel and their parents are able to convey that they have heard them fully. No lecture will get through, no reconciliation will be accomplished until the feelings are fully expressed and understood.

• Ask questions. This draws out the thoughts and feelings of our teens. Perhaps it has been your experience, as it has been mine, that what you really think and feel is not clear, even to you, until you've had a chance to express yourself to a trusted friend who will hear you out, blow away the chaff, forget the silly parts, and credit you with the best of what you have been able to conclude. That is the kind of friend our teens need in us.

• Avoid judging. Judging, as I am using the term, is pronouncing a sentence before all the facts are in. It's an attitude of condemnation. It's being *against* the other person rather than *for* him. If you are like the rest of us, you hate to be judged. After all, who but God knows you well enough—your deepest thoughts and full intentions—to make a valid judgment? Teens hate to be judged too. Judging blocks the flow of communication. It prevents the full expression of our teen's perspective.

• Listen. Sometimes our teens may ask our advice on certain matters, but they really want us to just listen. They want a sounding board. They want someone to whom they can entrust their thoughts and feelings. Thus, our first response to strong emotion in our teens ought to be to listen intently. Instead of immediately giving our opinion on what has been said, we listen. We use the skills discussed in chapter four to turn that ball around, to understand how the issue looks from our teen's perspective.

Warning! Seeing "the other side" is not easy. Contrary to the tennis ball illustration, issues between parents and teens are never totally black and white. Numerous shades of meaning are involved, and we must try to get as close as possible to the shade they see.

M = MOTIVATE RECONCILIATION

What happens if emotions have gotten out of hand and in our anger we have said some things that have really hurt our teenagers? Strategies alone are inadequate to deal effectively with hurt feelings. If the feeling of being wronged is not dealt with constructively, it plagues a relationship. It becomes a source of mistrust and friction. To lift the quality of parent-teen communication to a level which is relatively free of past mistakes and hurts, we need again to take the initiative, to be the first to bury the hatchet and motivate reconciliation. We need to ask the greatest healing question: *"Will you forgive me for my contribution to the problem?"*

When we ask this question, we are not admitting full blame for faulty communication. Rarely is any problem between two people the fault of only one of them. Normally, both contribute to the problem. The healing question, as stated above, works powerfully because both parties can say it honestly without feeling that one must bear the blame alone. When forgiveness is granted, there is an exhilarating feeling of freedom, of being able to start again, unshackled by the past.

Forgiving goes against the grain of our natural tendencies and it is for this reason that the question has such power. Lewis B. Smedes writes in a helpful book, *Forgive & Forget:* "Forgiving seems almost unnatural. Our sense of fairness tells us people should pay for the wrong they do. But forgiving is love's power to break nature's rule."[6]

A willingness to ask the greatest healing question influences the whole nature of our interactions with our teens. The quality of our communication will be *supportive* rather than *defensive.* In the following chart, notice the characteristics that produce defensiveness and those which convey support.

Quality of Communication

Defensive Characteristics	*Supportive Characteristics*
1. Evaluative—labels statements good or bad.	1. Descriptive—describes ideas without judgment.
2. Control—attempts to control the person or conversation.	2. Mutual—allows equal time for expression.
3. Self-centered—focuses only on one's own perspective.	3. Other-centered—focuses on understanding.
4. Attitude of superiority—condescends to the other person.	4. Attitude of equality—aims at achieving empathy.

Basic to our human needs is the forgiveness and support of at least one person significant to us. If we convey those qualities to our children, we take the biggest step toward responding effectively to strong emotions.

L = LEARN VERBAL SELF-DEFENSE

Some teens develop a mean streak. They will say whatever is calculated to hurt. The reason for their verbal attacks may range from feelings of inferiority to a perverted need for power. The reason might even be a chemical imbalance, like low blood sugar. But whatever the cause, they can become expert at finding the tender place and making their parents squirm.

Often parents with mean teens feel guilty about their teens' behavior and blame themselves. They become more and more compliant in hopes that compliance will solve the problem. They reason that the meanness is just a stage and that by ignoring the problem, eventually it will go away.

Sometimes the problem does go away. But even if verbal attacks from teens reflect a temporary stage, should parents have to endure the pain? Parents are not doormats. They don't need to let their daughters and sons wipe their feet on them or abuse them verbally. Being a good parent doesn't require us to be dummies.

We can defend ourselves verbally in effective ways. Our aim is not to counterattack, yell, get revenge, or escalate a verbal war. It is simply to teach our teens that no one—not our business associates, not our neighbors, and not our children—has the right to inflict verbal damage upon us.

Effective verbal defense can easily be learned if we keep in mind the following principles.

• Take charge. The parent is in charge, the president of the family "firm." Quietly exercise the authority that is yours. Don't try to *prove* your superiority by getting into power struggles. *Assume* it. It is necessary to realize internally your rightful place as a parent.

• Don't shout. Strength is shown by a firm quiet assertiveness, not in yelling or becoming belligerent. Yelling is a sign that you have lost control. It's counterproductive.

• Model behavior. Teens tend to do what we do, so it is

important to commit ourselves to treating them as we would want to be treated. View any verbal defense as a teaching tool that our teens can develop and use when needed in their own interpersonal relationships.

• Love yourself. Adopt a conscious and healthy self-esteem. You have God-given dignity and worth and no one can take that from you. Refuse to accept a low opinion of yourself. Let no one intimidate you—not even your children.

Let's apply these principles to common forms of verbal attack.

Putdowns

Teen: You don't want to make my lunch because you're too lazy!

Ineffective Defense	*Effective Defense*
Parent: I'm not the one who's lazy. It's you! You never do anything around here!	Parent: (lightly) I wish I had the *time* to be lazy. The fact is, I have more than I can do in the time I have. (seriously) I feel put down when you attach a negative label to my request. Let's not do that to each other. I need your help.

Defiance

Teen: I will not take out the garbage! That's Bob's job.

Ineffective Defense	*Effective Defense*
Parent: Oh yes you will! You will do what I tell you to do, you ungrateful child!	Parent: Bob is mowing a lawn. Our guests will be here in a half hour. I need your help.

Threats

Teen: I'll show you. I'll leave home and get my own apartment somewhere.

Ineffective Defense	*Effective Defense*
Parent: No! Don't do that! You don't know what you are doing! It'll kill me to think of you roaming the streets! What will people say? Go ahead and do what you want. But please come home!	Parent: John, I don't want you to leave. But if you insist, I can't stop you.

Frustration

Teen: I'm sick and tired of you telling me what to do! I'm 16, for heaven's sake! Get off my back!

Ineffective Response	*Effective Response*
Parent: I'm sick and tired of having to tell you a hundred times to do what any responsible 16-year-old would already be doing!	Parent: Kim, I really dislike telling you what to do, too. Yet, for this family to function smoothly, some things have to be done that are not being done. How do you suggest we solve this problem?

Y = YIELD WHEN YOUR TEEN IS RIGHT

Suppose you and your teen have had an argument and you begin to realize that your teen is right. Some new piece of information has come into the discussion that you had missed before. What can you say? Is it ever right for a parent to yield to a teen? If so, what happens to parental authority?

Think about your reactions to your parents when you knew you were right. How did you feel about your parents when they maintained their position out of stubborn pride or refusal to see the evidence? Did you have more or less respect for them? What did you wish they would do?

I remember feeling a sense of euphoria when my father would say, "Son, I think you're right" or "Paul, I guess I made a mistake." Sometimes the euphoria resulted from the feeling that I had won a personal victory, that even as a teen I had something to say that made sense, that I could talk on an adult level and make some valid points. It made me feel very good about myself. But usually the euphoria was based on more than that. It was a sense that my father had won a victory, too . . . a victory over stubborn pride, having to prove he was always right. He was strong and secure enough to admit mistakes and I respected him for it.

* * * * *

My wife and I realize that in responding to strong emotions, we can't take the necessary steps solely in our own power. That's why we find ourselves praying prayers like this one by Peter Marshall:

> Lord, when we are wrong, make us willing to change. And when we are right, make us easy to live with.[7]

ACTION STEPS FOR POSITIVE COMMUNICATION

1. Think of some recent conversation with your teen when you found it difficult to control your responses. Write down how you intend to handle a similar situation the next time it occurs.

2. What can you do to avoid vicious cycles of hurtful remarks with your teen? Discuss with your teen how the patterns seem to develop and work on a plan that you both agree will work when you are angry with each other.

3. What three strategies in the section on "Listen to the Teen Perspective" do you think would be most helpful in communicating with your teen? Make at least one of them a goal and begin implementing that goal today.

4. If someone asked you the "greatest healing question," what effect do you think it would have on you? Plan to ask your teen that question whenever there are hurt feelings because of something you said or did.

5. Reflect on some verbal attack you received from your teen and write it down. Then write a brief defense that follows the guidelines in the section, "Learn Verbal Self-Defense."

6. Suppose you get in an argument about your teen watching TV because you assume he has not done his homework. Then you discover that you were wrong. Write down what you would say to your teen.

> Youth today have detestable manners, flout authority, and have no respect for their elders. What kind of awful creatures will they be when they grow up?
>
> Socrates, 399 B.C.

7

Parental Authority: The Art of Saying No . . . and Yes!

Even before Socrates, the Greek poet Hesiod wrote in 800 B.C., "I see no hope for the future of our people if they are dependent on the frivolous youth of today, for certainly all youth are reckless beyond words." Perhaps our problem is not quite as bad as all that.

In every age, parents of teens have been concerned about how to exercise their authority. The old rules that worked with younger children seem not to apply during adolescence. At a parenting seminar, I asked the parents of adolescents to write down their concerns about exercising their authority. Here are a few.

- Finding a consequence that can be enforced.
- Being worn out with complaints from my teenager about my decisions.
- Being consistent and following through with what I say I'm going to do.

— Coming on too strong, being too harsh.
— Knowing what the real boundaries should be. (When I figure that out, my husband changes them!)
— Fearing "the argument." I lack the authority to say No and have that accepted.
— Speaking too quickly and saying No, then feeling the need to change my decision.
— Reacting emotionally before thinking through my response.
— Giving in too soon and giving up.

The only way to manage a perplexing array of parental concerns is to discover the relevant principles and use them. These fundamental laws make it unnecessary to reinvent the wheel every time a new problem arises. They are few enough to remember and broad enough to be useful in numerous situations. Applying six principles related to parental authority will prevent us from making too many mistakes and will increase our chances of saying No and Yes effectively.

PRINCIPLE 1: MAKE DECISIONS BASED ON GOALS

Without a standard by which to make decisions, parents are lost in confusion, inconsistency, and not knowing what to say next. Goals provide parents a reference point for choosing appropriate words and actions. Goals guide our communication in the direction we want it to go. I find the following goal helpful.

To train my children how to make wise decisions and take full responsibility for their choices.

Let's test this goal. As you read each of the following options that are available to us as parents, answer the question, Will this action help me reach the parenting goal above? Write *yes* or *no* in front of each item:

N 1. Set out our teens' clothes for the next day.
N 2. Wake up our teens every morning.
N 3. Make job appointments for our teens.

_____ 4. Say, "Do this because I said so."

___N___ 5. Suggest that when our teens oversleep, they tell their teachers they are sick so that they won't get an F for the day.

___Y___ 6. Ask our teens what they think the solution is to a problem we face at work.

___Y___ 7. Ask what our teens would do if someone tried to sell them a term paper they could turn in as their own.

___Y___ 8. Ask our teens what the consequences of a certain action would be.

___Y___ 9. Explore with our teens alternative solutions to a problem and the long-range consequences.

___Y___ 10. Say No, give reasons, and remain firm about an action that is not acceptable to us.

When measured against a goal, a course of action usually becomes clear instantly. A goal can decrease the chances of inconsistency and not knowing what to do.

When we set goals for the development of our teens, it's important to talk about them with our teenagers. They need to know that we appreciate their built-in drive for independence, that we want them to become fully functioning, mature adults. For some teens, the shift to independence can't happen fast enough. They may need help to see the long view, to notice that they really are making progress toward adulthood.

When Jud turned sixteen, I mentioned to him that I was pleased to see him taking more responsibility for his behavior and me taking less. He had just received his driver's license and was allowed to drive the car on his own—an event that signaled a new level of maturity and independence. I told him he had earned it.

Then I showed him the simple diagram on the following page. Jud's comment was: "Dad, it's not exactly right. The lines of authority and independence are never straight. They go up and down. Freedom is not given evenly through adolescence. Sometimes a parent gives freedom and then needs to take it away." He's right. There *is* a lot of give-and-take in the testing of privilege and responsibility. We decided that the graph still might be useful in showing the *general* direction and shift of authority and independence.

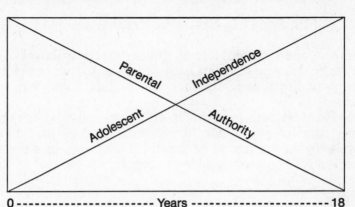

We also discussed that as the lines of parental authority and teenage independence approach each other, there is bound to be more conflict and confusion than usual. We can expect it. We must remember too that the transfer of control is inevitable and healthy.

I am helped by thinking of this transition as a shift in parental roles from a position of decision maker to that of consultant.

Parental Decision Maker (Childhood and early teens)	*Parental Consultant* (Middle and late teens)
1. Makes most decisions	1. Guides decisions
2. Bears major responsibility	2. Shares responsibility
3. Has control	3. Has influence
4. Acts on information	4. Provides information

You may want to clarify (in writing) your own parental goals, especially your goal regarding the growing independence of your teen. Commit yourself to it so that it can guide you toward the role of parental consultant. Talk enthusiastically about it so that your teenager knows your rules and regulations are not arbitrary, unfair, or meaningless, but designed rather to bring him or her to full maturity and independence as an adult in due time.

PRINCIPLE 2: BUILD RELATIONSHIP POWER

One mother complained: "I have no control over my son anymore. He's bigger than I am and knows I can't hurt him. I talk until I'm blue in the face, but he just does whatever he wants."

Parental authority, to be effective, must be backed by some form of power. Dr. Tom Elkin, head of the Christian Psychological Center in Memphis, Tennessee, says there are four kinds of power available to parents:

1. Physical
2. Intellectual
3. Material
4. Relational

Early in a child's life, we may use physical force, reasoning, and the giving or withholding of tangible rewards as forms of power. But in the long run, there is no way that we can win a power struggle with older children through these means. By the teenage years, the most effective form of parental power will be centered in the *relationship* between the parent and the teenager.

Relational power is positive. It's a force within our teens based on respect rather than fear. It is built by listening intently, by looking at their side of the issue as well as our own, by spending time with them, by letting them know of our love for them. Relational power does not mean the absence of discipline or the refusal to apply logical consequences when necessary. It includes them. What it precludes is the need to resort to threats, insults, yelling, and physical force. Of course, relational power is not always effective. But over a period of time, building a strong relationship with our teens provides the best framework for achieving our parenting goals.

PRINCIPLE 3: CHOOSE AN EFFECTIVE PARENTING STYLE

On the basis of a careful study, researcher Diana Baumrind identified three types of parental styles related to discipline and demonstrated how each pattern shapes the child in a different way.[1]

1. *Authoritarian* or *autocratic* parents favor punitive or forceful methods to curb the self-will of a child. Negotiation or verbal give-and-take is discouraged because autocratic parents expect their children to believe parents are always right. The autocratic approach to power is linked more to the feelings than the thoughts of the parent. It is more a reaction to stress and frustration than an expression of long-term parental goals.

According to another study of 7,050 high school youth by Strommen and Strommen, the effect of parental over-control on youth was lower self-esteem and strong feelings of self-condemnation. The study indicated that adolescents living under autocratic control were likely to be characterized by the following behaviors: hostility toward parents, antisocial activities, feelings of social alienation, rejection of traditional moral standards, and the inability to relate well to people.[2]

2. *Permissive* parents think of themselves as resources to be used as the child wishes—not as involved mothers and fathers responsible for shaping the child's future behavior. They want their children to be free of restraint and to develop as they choose. Permissiveness is sometimes seen as a form of rejection. The effect of undercontrol may cause teens to feel that their parents really don't care about them. Said one teenager in California,

> Why does it always have to be my decision?
> Why can't my dad just say, "You can't go"?
> I think that if somebody really loves you,
> they don't just let you do whatever you want.[3]

According to Strommen and Strommen, adolescents of permissive parents show one or more of the following characteristics: unlikely to go out of their way to help people, less willing to live by the moral standards of their parents, more likely to become involved in the use and abuse of alcohol, sex, and drugs, and less likely to relate well to others or be religiously and ethically motivated.[4]

3. *Authoritative* or *democratic* parents combine a firm, flexible authority with a healthy amount of freedom in parenting. The authoritative parent affirms a child's unique personality and way of approaching things, but at the same time holds the child accountable to standards for behavior, attitudes, conversation, and the quality of their relationship.

Authoritative parents give their children the chance to talk over rules that they do not like or understand. As a result of talking them over, the parents may modify the rules if there is good reason to do so, but they do not just give in to whatever the child or teenager wants.

On the basis of her research of preschool children, Baumrind concludes that authoritative patterns are more beneficial to children than autocratic and permissive patterns.[5] On the basis of their study of young adolescents, the Strommens came to the same conclusion. They found the teenagers of authoritative parents to be more service-oriented, concerned about people, free from feelings of alienation, and committed to a religious faith.[6]

A striking illustration of the contrasting effects of parental approaches is seen in a study of the use of marijuana by college students. The findings showed high use of marijuana by students of permissive parents, medium use by students who viewed their parents as autocratic, and low use by students who viewed their parents as democratic.[7]

If our parenting styles have been less than effective, we can begin now to make the changes we want to make. It is important not to continually blame ourselves for the mistakes we have made. The past is over and done. Now, in the present, we can ask forgiveness for our part in any problem and choose in the days ahead to practice as well as we can an effective parenting style.

PRINCIPLE 4: DISCIPLINE WITH RESPECT

Most parents would agree that teenagers still are in need of discipline, but they often confuse *discipline* with *punishment*. They are not the same. Punishment includes angry words or actions that are punitive, insensitive, and insulting. Discipline, on the other hand, refers to words and actions that instruct, train, and correct. Discipline comes from the same root word as disciple, which means "learner." Discipline involves the positive use of parental authority to bring about desired change.

Psychologist Bruce Narramore, in his book, *Adolescence Is Not an Illness,* shows the difference between discipline and punishment in a way I find very helpful:[8]

	Punishment	Discipline
Purpose	Justice, or to inflict penalty for an offense	Promote maturity and growth
Focus	Past misdeeds	Future correct attitudes and actions
Attitude of Parent Figure	Anger	Love
Resulting Behavior	Conformity or rebellion	Growth
Resulting Emotion	Fear, guilt, or anger	Love and security

Let's apply this concept of discipline to the following situation.

Situation

A teenager comes home an hour after curfew even though parent and teen have discussed the need to respect the curfew.

| *Punishment Approach* | *Discipline Approach* |

Punishment Approach

Parent: (with anger) You're really in trouble now! I told you to be home an hour ago! You're grounded for the next month!

Teen: But Dad, I was . . . .

Parent: (yelling) You were late! One whole hour late!

Teen: But I can explain . . . .

Parent: I don't want to hear it! You always seem to make up a story. You can't handle responsibility. You don't even know how to come home on time.

Teen: (yelling back) That's not fair! Were you ever late? Did you ever make a mistake? Would you ever admit it if you did?

Discipline Approach

Parent: (firmly) Son, what happened?

Teen: Dad, we went out to get something to eat after the game and I just lost track of the time.

Parent: I can understand how that can happen. But we had a firm agreement. I feel somewhat betrayed when our agreements are broken.

Teen: I know, Dad. I'm sorry.

Parent: I forgive you son. Since this is not the first time, there will be a consequence. You will be grounded for a week as a reminder of the importance of our agreement.

Comment: In the punishment approach, there is little real communication and little incentive for the teenager to make positive change. The father's anger produces anger, defensiveness, sarcasm, and a strain on the relationship. In the discipline approach, the father chooses to withhold judgment, ask (2) for information, keep the communication going at a rational (3) level, disclose his own feelings, draw upon his relationship (5) (4) power, and exert his authority in a way that will likely motivate positive change.

I am aware that most of us will occasionally become angry with our teenagers and resort to words that do not typify our intention to discipline with respect. Often the cause of such angry responses does not stem from our teens, although they can be masterfully obnoxious, but from us—from our own past failures, our frustrations of the day, our worries about tomorrow, and our discouragement over not reaching our expectations. There is no cure-all to prevent failures and mistakes, but there is a revitalizing force available to the believer: forgiveness. When we know we are forgiven, we can more readily choose to try again.

PRINCIPLE 5: SAY NO CALMLY

"OK," you say, "I'll try again. But how do I stay calm when I have to say No to my teen and my teen starts yelling at me? How do I stay calm when everything around me is in a state of chaos and I am made to feel that I'm the reason everyone is upset?"

Fair questions. Let's assume we intend to operate on the first four principles:

1. Make decisions based on goals.
2. Build relationship power.
3. Choose an effective parenting style.
4. Discipline with respect.

To effectively handle challenges to our authority, we now need to add the fifth principle: Say No calmly. This principle involves skills that will help us implement our parental authority. Because skills can become habits, these skills are especially helpful when our normal resilience and tolerance are low. They can function without a great deal of conscious thought once they have been committed to memory and practice.

• *Use the "No Sandwich."* Say No when necessary, but sandwich it between two cushioning statements that help to soften the blow of a negative response. This softening effect is important because often our teens hear a No response as a rejection of them personally or a challenge to their "rights." The first cushioning layer is a statement that acknowledges that we really heard what our teens said or asked. This precludes our teens from thinking that our No means that we must not have understood. It diminishes the tendency to engage in a long defense or debate of their position. Next comes the No response or "meat" of the sandwich. Here we simply state our refusal and why we will not or cannot comply with their wishes. After the No, there is another cushioning statement about something we will do or can say to ease the sting of the refusal.

1. I understand that you want to borrow the Buick for your date Friday night.
2. But I need the car myself Friday night for a meeting that I have downtown.
3. I will be happy to let you drive the Ford. You can use the Buick next Friday if you let me know soon enough.

* * * * *

1. I know that you want me to agree with you.
2. But I see the issue from a different point of view.
3. I acknowledge your right to your point of view and I hope you will acknowledge the same right for me.

* * * * *

1. I understand that you want to go to the party at Pete's house.
2. But the answer is No because we both know there have been drugs at other parties Pete has had.
3. I would be happy for you to have a party for your

friends at our house. I am willing to help you prepare the food if you want me to.

• *Try the "Broken Record" Technique.* If you have tried the "No Sandwich" and your teen persists in trying to control you or get you to change your mind, you can stay relaxed and simply repeat No or a one-sentence refusal in a calm but firm voice until the message gets through. For example, you could repeat, "My decision is that for the reasons I stated, you cannot go to the party." Since you do not need to generate new reasons with this technique, you can concentrate on maintaining a calm, firm voice. Do not insult your teen with a response like "Are you deaf?" Don't use sarcasm or a disgusted tone of voice because then the teen is challenged to react not only to his disappointment, but also to the feeling that he is being attacked.

• *Deal with Principle, Not Pressure.* Your principles, values, or goals help you know when to say No and when to say Yes. It may take some time and effort to clarify them in your own mind. But once you have established them, it is relatively easy to say No (or Yes) on the basis of your principles. Do not yield to pressure. If you do, you will teach your teen to keep on exerting pressure in greater amounts until you give in. For example, if it is your principle that your daughter not go on single dates until she is sixteen, discuss that principle with her early, before the issue even comes up. Explain why you hold to it. Discuss the options she has of double dating and group dating. Tell her that there may be times when she will not like that principle, but because you believe it is reasonable and well founded, you will stick to it. Let her know you are not afraid to say No on principle and that you will not yield to pressure. In so doing, you will teach her the valuable lesson of doing the same.

• *Practice Calm Responses.* It might not be your temperament to respond calmly. You might view each argument or new option your teen brings up as a challenge to your parental authority. It might be true that you experience some payoff when you get angry and raise your voice. For example, releasing the tension in this way might make you feel better. Your teen might seem to listen to you more attentively and comply with your wishes when you yell. But do you want your teen to respond to you the same way? The proverb is true, "anger begets anger." If you want to try calm responses, commit yourself to practicing them. It could take *a lot of practice* because your teen might be "programmed" to respond only when you are angry. You will need to tell your teen that you are changing your style of responding. Explain why. Say that it will be a mistake to interpret your calmness as a lack of commitment or as indecisiveness. Enlist your teen's cooperation if possible. Then practice the variety of ways a calm No can be expressed:

I have decided the answer is No. Don't pressure me.

＊ ＊ ＊ ＊ ＊

I know this is important to you and I would like to say Yes to you if I could, but I can't. The answer is No.

＊ ＊ ＊ ＊ ＊

It might be true that all the other boys your age are drinking. But you're not "all the other boys." You are you. And you are my son. For the reasons we discussed, the answer is No.

＊ ＊ ＊ ＊ ＊

I am willing to negotiate with you whenever I can. But this is not one of those times. The answer is No.

＊ ＊ ＊ ＊ ＊

Right now I am very tired and frustrated. I will explain my reasons for saying No after I get some rest.

Saying No calmly works. It trains your teen to take responsibility seriously because you do. It strengthens your relationship with your teen because it communicates that you are willing to risk standing up for something you believe in—your teen. It disciplines with respect. And it's one way of affirming your teen.

PRINCIPLE 6: AFFIRM YOUR TEEN

Saying No must never become a habit. Whenever possible we need to affirm our teens with votes of confidence, with a willingness to let them try their wings and sometimes fail.

My wife and I say Yes to anything that will help build healthy self-esteem in our children. We want them to be psychologically strong, to believe that they have inherent worth and dignity whatever anyone else may tell them. We want them to believe that they can do their work well and that they have the capacity to achieve their own worthwhile personal goals.

We say Yes to their growing ability to handle responsibility. We actively work at encouraging our children to develop inner controls and positive disciplines rather than merely conforming to external controls.

We say Yes to their desire to relate skillfully to other people. We want our children to feel comfortable with their peers and with adults. We talk about what attitudes and behaviors are required to develop these skills and try to model them as best we can. We talk about our own mistakes in this area too and what we have tried to do to correct them.

We say Yes to our children's right to say No. We want them to develop the courage to say No to anyone who tries to pressure them to do something that they know is wrong. We want them to say No to their own feelings of intimidation, fear, or worthlessness. We want them to know how to say No to lifestyles that, however popular or tempting, conflict with what they know to be right and true.

We say Yes to their efforts to show kindness, courtesy, and love to other people—even when it costs us time and money.

We say Yes to any worthwhile talents or skills they want to develop: piano, banjo, guitar, horseback riding, tennis, riding a unicycle, running cross-country.

We say Yes to forgiving them and forgetting past mistakes.

We say Yes to their need for an adequate foundation for life, a world and life view that encompasses the best for them in the physical, social, mental, emotional, moral, and spiritual dimensions of their lives. For our family, that foundation is faith in Jesus Christ.

ACTION STEPS FOR POSITIVE COMMUNICATION

1. Think about what your real goal is for the development of your teenager. Then write it down. Revise it until you are satisfied that it represents the direction you want to go as a parent. Complete the sentence: My goal is to _____
_____ .

2. List three things you will do this week to build the relational power you have with your teen (e.g., go to a sporting event, shopping, or out for a hamburger together).

    a.
    b.
    c.

3. Which of the three parenting styles discussed in this chapter comes closest to your own? What could you do to increase the effectiveness of your parenting style?

4. Put yourself in the position of your teenager for a moment. From the tone of your voice and the words you use, how would you describe the way you come across to your teenager? List three adjectives that describe how your teen might feel.

    a.
    b.
    c.

5. Try using the "No Sandwich" technique in response to your daughter's request to drive the car alone even though her driver's permit restricts her to drive only with an adult in the car.

    Cushion statement _____ .
    The No statement _____ .
    Cushion statement _____ .

6. With regard to the five areas of development discussed in chapter two (Physical, Social, Mental, Emotional, Moral/ Spiritual), in what area do you feel your teen needs the most affirmation? _____
What is one thing you can say that will affirm your teen in that area? _____ .

Better a patient man than a warrior, a
man who controls his temper than one
who takes a city.[1]

Solomon

How Temperament
Influences
Communication

Growing up in a family with five sisters (no brothers!), I
had plenty of opportunity to observe a fascinating array of
temperaments at work. One sister enjoyed being in charge (we
knew early that she would be a schoolteacher). Another found
humor in almost everything (we knew she would add happiness to any group). Two demonstrated a great deal of patience
and interest in other people (we knew one would be fit for
nursing and the other for counseling). Another loved to clean
up after everyone (we knew she would be a great organizer).

Temperament refers to behavioral style, an inborn disposition to act and think and talk in certain ways. Since only
seven percent of what we convey to another person is strictly
related to our words, our temperaments have a major influence
on our communication patterns.

Solomon suggests that controlling one's temper, or temperament, is better than winning a military victory. It may also
seem more difficult. Often it is hard to restrain emotions and

adjust the way we express ourselves. It may be simpler to "blow the other person away" with the full force of our fury. But when we lose our tempers, emotions such as anger are no longer "tempered" by traits such as patience and self-control. The result is damaged relationships.

To temper our natural impulses and to gain the control necessary for optimum communication, we need to understand how our temperaments affect our teenagers and how we "come across" to them. Then we can diminish the negative effects of our weaknesses and make the most of our strengths.

UNDERSTANDING TEMPERAMENTS

Hippocrates (460–370 B.C.), the "father of medicine," theorized that there were four basic fluids within the body of each person which determined how a person acted. He claimed that people could be classified on the basis of these fluids as either Choleric, Sanguine, Phlegmatic, or Melancholy. (I prefer to designate these traits according to their dominant characteristics as Pragmatic, Extrovert, Amiable, and Analytical.) While Hippocrates' idea that body fluids produced certain temperaments proved unscientific, the observation of four basic temperaments has persisted through the ages and is used today as a convenient tool for self-understanding.[2]

Although parents are well aware that there are differences from one child to the next, most of us have not received any real help in discerning what those differences are or how to respond to them.

Understanding ourselves better helps us to "temper" tendencies in our communication patterns that create misunderstanding and hurt feelings in our teenagers. The analysis is not hard to do. In fact, it really is intriguing because it allows us to get a better grip on who we are and how to communicate what we mean to others.

The following inventory is not intended to be a scientific instrument, nor a test with right or wrong answers. Its purpose is to generate insights about our temperaments by causing us to reflect on a number of behavioral styles. For each item, place a numerical value that best represents the *frequency* of each behavioral style in the context of the family

(1 = seldom, 2 = sometimes, 3 = often, 4 = usually). You may ask your spouse and teenager to take this inventory or you can estimate the appropriate number for them:

Section 1

Husband	Wife	Teen	
——	——	——	Sets very high standards for self; expects to meet them.
——	——	——	Is a leader in the family; likes to take charge.
——	——	——	Wants to see immediate responses to requests or instructions.
——	——	——	Solves problems.
——	——	——	Makes quick decisions about what should or should not be done.
——	——	——	Is insensitive to feelings.
——	——	——	Becomes impatient with others.
——	——	——	Is viewed by others as inflexible, unyielding.
——	——	——	Reacts without knowing all the facts.
——	——	——	Becomes autocratic or overbearing when under tension.
——	——	——	Totals

Section 2

Husband	Wife	Teen	
——	——	——	Makes home a fun place to be.
——	——	——	Is well liked by peers.
——	——	——	Talks easily and often.
——	——	——	Quickly sees the funny or humorous side of things.
——	——	——	Lives in the present and the future, not the past.
——	——	——	Is easily angered.
——	——	——	Talks more than listens.
——	——	——	Is perceived to use manipulation in controlling others.
——	——	——	Lacks self-discipline.
——	——	——	Verbally attacks others when under stress.
——	——	——	Totals

Section 3

Husband	Wife	Teen	
——	——	——	Is motivated by relationships.
——	——	——	Looks for ways to support or encourage family.
——	——	——	Tends to agree with family.
——	——	——	Demonstrates a great deal of patience.

——	——	—— Listens carefully to what family says.
——	——	—— Conforms to family's wishes and plans.
——	——	—— Tends not to confront members of the family.
——	——	—— Dislikes initiating conversation.
——	——	—— Misses opportunities to share deep feelings.
——	——	—— Gives in to keep the peace.
——	——	—— Totals

Section 4

Husband Wife Teen

——	——	—— Is motivated by the need to be right.
——	——	—— Checks the accuracy of what the family says.
——	——	—— Concentrates on details.
——	——	—— Thinks things through before giving an answer.
——	——	—— Is good at creating solutions to problems.
——	——	—— Is hard to please.
——	——	—— Is hesitant or indecisive when situations need an immediate response.
——	——	—— Tends not to express emotion or enthusiasm in front of the family.
——	——	—— Relates to the family primarily at the level of thought rather than feeling.
——	——	—— Avoids confronting problems whenever possible.
——	——	—— Totals

To score this inventory, add your column in each section. Find the section with your highest score and compare it with the list of temperaments below. (Each person taking the inventory should do the same.)

Section 1 *Pragmatic* (Emphasis on getting things done.)   M

Section 2 *Extrovert* (Emphasis on influencing others.)

Section 3 *Amiable* (Emphasis on achieving cooperation.)   H⊆

Section 4 *Analytical* (Emphasis on order.)

Keep in mind three important points about temperaments. First, although one temperament is normally dominant, none of us reveals the traits or characteristics of just one temperament. Usually we demonstrate a blend of two, maybe three. Second, we tend to change the way we express ourselves depending on the context. Certain traits will be dominant in the work environment, others will be more apparent in the home. Third, whatever the context, each temperament has strengths and weaknesses that reveal themselves in communication.

TEMPERAMENT COMMUNICATION PATTERNS

In the following charts, we will examine how the four basic temperaments tend to interact with each other and how temperament communication patterns can cause misunderstanding. The charts guide us to consider changes in our

If you are	And your teen is	Your patterns that may cause problems include	Actions needed:
		Section 1	
Pragmatic	Pragmatic	Over-controlling; not allowing adequate freedom.	Restrain tendency to overcontrol a situation.
	Extrovert	Over-concern for results; not enough attention to motivation.	Reduce stress on results; increase ability to laugh.
	Amiable	Not taking enough time to listen and build a quality relationship.	Take time to listen.
	Analytical	Too quick to make decisions; not thorough enough.	Slow down; pay attention to detail.
		Section 2	
Extrovert	Pragmatic	Under-concern for results; too emotional.	Acknowledge teen's desire for results.
	Extrovert	Grandstanding; calling too much attention to yourself.	Allow teen to be the life of the party.
	Amiable	Quickness in thinking or talking; not enough depth relationship.	Work at listening and responding to teen's feelings.
	Analytical	Lack of attention to detail; impulsive tendencies.	Be more careful; think about what you say.

communication patterns that could produce stronger relationships and better understanding. The response some experience from the study of charts like these is, "Aha! That's what I've been doing wrong. This is what I need to do."

Note: *Weaknesses are often strengths pushed to the extreme.* For example, the ability to make quick decisions

If you are	And your teen is	Your patterns that may cause problems include	Actions needed:
		Section 3	
Amiable	Pragmatic	Too much small talk; not enough decisive action.	Reduce amount of talk; get to the bottom line.
	Extrovert	Apparent lack of quickness; not enough focus on the present.	Increase your quickness in responding.
	Amiable	Lack of initiative; waiting too long for your teen to initiate talk.	Take initiative in talking; ask questions.
	Analytical	Over-concern about relationship; not enough task orientation.	Increase your interest in your teen's tasks.
		Section 4	
Analytical	Pragmatic	Slowness to make decisions; too methodical.	Respond quicker.
	Extrovert	Too much attention to details; not enough humor.	Relax more. Be more cheerful.
	Amiable	Not letting your teen know how you feel; insensitivity to feelings.	Strive for openness; express your feelings.
	Analytical	Arguing about who is more correct; unhealthy introspection.	Allow your teen differences of opinion.

sometimes results in wrong assumptions; a sense of humor may repress deep feelings. I like the idea that weaknesses may be strengths taken a bit too far because it seems a lot easier to pull back and refine a strength than to overcome a weakness. It makes working to improve a temperament communication pattern a positive task, the task of expressing our best selves more often. As we identify the patterns that cause us trouble, we can begin the process of controlling them.

STRATEGIES FOR UNDERSTANDING

• *Accept the differences in temperaments.* Although you and your teen might have similar temperaments, the chances are good that you might not. That's OK. Beware of putting your teen in a box, of categorizing him or her in ways that don't allow the expression of distinguishing traits. Unless we realize that differences in temperaments are legitimate, we may fall into the trap of wanting our teens to be carbon copies of ourselves. Our teens need to be accepted as individuals. Acceptance will make them feel more at ease, less defensive, and more accepting of the character traits they might not like in us.

• *Beware of selective perception.* Temperaments can cause us to view our teens through filters that block out a realistic picture. Schoolteachers and police officers complain that some parents refuse to see or believe negative behavior patterns in their teenagers. It's always somebody else's fault—not their teen's. But temperament filters can also prevent us from seeing strengths in our teens. If you are pragmatic and your teen is amiable, you may not fully appreciate the value of your teen's ability to establish strong friendships. When we understand the strengths inherent in our teens' temperaments, we can relate to their strengths and draw out the best in them. Further, we will avoid the temptation to expect our teenagers to express themselves just like we do. We will be less likely to project our temperament onto them and thus will be able to convey greater understanding and acceptance of our teens as they are.

• *Increase your versatility.* If the chart revealed some temperament tendencies that you feel might be the cause of communication breakdowns with your teen, begin to widen the range of your responses to your teen in a way that your

teen will appreciate and that will promote greater understanding. Versatility increases options for knowing how to
respond in any situation, and the more options available, the
better chance we have to choose a communicative style that
will enhance understanding.

    • *Practice open communication.* Conflicts arise when
misunderstanding is not dealt with properly. Open communication gets to the heart of issues. It is not defensive. It makes
us unafraid to risk the fact that our teens might not like what
we say. Open communication is being honest, straightforward, truthful. Certainly it uses good judgment and tact, but
open communication builds on the fact that our teens want to
know how we feel and what we think. It lets our teens know
who we really are. Yes, it does provide a clear target at which
they can aim their rebuttal. But it is so much better than the
alternatives of avoidance and suppression because it yields
understanding.

THE NEED FOR PARENTAL TEAMWORK

    In families where the mother and father are present, both
need to think about how they can make their unique temperaments and conversational styles work together rather than
against each other. Husband and wife likely see issues from
very different viewpoints. Each has different skills and abilities. One may be a better talker; the other a better listener. One
may have the time management skills of a Pragmatist; the other
the discernment of an Analytical Thinker. These differences
could lead parents to compete, to argue, to forget who the real
opponents are. Or the differences could enable parents to see
their need for each other and work together as a team. I find
that parental teamwork is helped immeasurably when my wife
Janiece and I follow three rules.

    First, agree on basic parenting principles. Janiece and I
often approach our parenting tasks from different viewpoints
based on our temperaments. Her temperament is Pragmatic/
Extrovert. I am a mix between Amiable and Analytical. In order to work together as a team, we have had to think through
and talk extensively about the principles we want to use in
parenting our children. Here are a few that work for us:

— Don't yell. It's counterproductive.
— Build self-esteem daily.
— Listen; ask questions first; act second.
— Speak the truth in love.
— Allow as much freedom as possible within reasonable boundaries.
— Accept differences in temperament.
— Be always ready to forgive.
— Support each other in the parenting role.

This last principle bears comment. Janiece and I don't always agree on how to solve a problem with the children. If we sense an important disagreement with each other developing in front of the children, we tell them that Mom and Dad need to talk over the matter and then we will discuss it with them or give them our decision. This is not dishonest; it's smart. Undermining each other's authority would be the first step toward loss of parental control. It would give a message to the children that they can take sides, that they can "divide and conquer." In the matter of parenting our children, it's more important to be unified than it is to be "right."

Second, compensate for your spouse's weaknesses. If my wife and I were both alike, one of us would be unnecessary. But I need her help and she needs mine. Because of that fact, we both fight against any tendency to criticize the other because we know by experience that road leads nowhere. Instead we try to compensate for each other's weaknesses, to fill in the gaps.

Without Janiece, a lot of tasks that the children really need to learn would be overlooked by me. Their chores would not get done. Without me, differences in the children's temperaments would not be as readily discerned and the principle above (about listening, then acting) would get turned around. By compensating for each other's weaknesses, we are able to work better as a team.

Third, draw out your spouse's strengths. Within each of us are strengths still in raw form. They include traits of character, attitudes, beliefs, values, and ways of communicating that enhance self-esteem and make conversation mutually pleasing and stimulating. On the other hand, just the opposite may occur and we surprise ourselves with our pettiness, meanness, and lack of sensitivity.

To change negative habits of personality and communication, most of us need help. Few are in a better position to help us than our spouses. When they focus their attention on the best in us, they set in motion the law of positive reinforcement. That is, when we are supported in an area of strength, we are encouraged to make the effort and take the time necessary to build upon that strength, to increase its frequency, to try again when we fail. Happily, it works that way for our spouses, too.

ACTION STEPS FOR POSITIVE COMMUNICATION

1. Review the section on "Understanding Temperament" and jot down four characteristics that describe you.

2. List strengths that you sometimes carry to an extreme.

3. Write down the actions needed (pp. 116–117) that seem most appropriate to your temperament traits. For example, one of the versatility steps I need to work on is to *face confrontation* when my son doesn't follow through on his responsibilities.

4. Use the basic parenting principles listed in "The Need for Parental Teamwork" as a stimulus to write your own principles for parenting. Encourage your spouse to do the same. Discuss them and work out a plan for implementing them as a team.

危 = Danger

機 = Opportunity

危 機 = Crisis

9

Confronting Major Problems

Just as the word crisis in Chinese includes both danger and opportunity, so does the period of adolescence. The opportunity results from an adolescent's new interest in basic concerns, such as a philosophy of life, the need for self-discipline, the relation of sex and marriage, and the purpose of our existence. But the danger is that others will exert an influence that could undermine the values we have tried to teach and turn our teens down a path that leads to destruction.

Psychologist David Elkind writes, "The epidemic of teenage problem behavior in America today is serious and frightening."[1] Because of the magnitude of the problems confronting our teenagers, they are highly vulnerable to certain dangers. Many parents do not understand the nature of these problems or how to deal with them. Yet, it is possible, with help, to beat the odds.

In this chapter, we look at four problem areas and what we can do to help our teenagers cope with the dangers in each.

Warning: some of the material in this chapter is explicit. It won't be easy to work through it or to implement solutions, but with help it is possible to minimize the dangers teenagers face and seize the opportunities. Let's dig in.

ROCK MUSIC PHILOSOPHIES

Is there any good in rock music? Smokey Robinson, lead singer of The Miracles, released an anti-drug song/video entitled, "Be Kind to the Growing Mind." Stevie Wonder did a popular song/video directed at teens entitled "Don't Drive Drunk." Billy Joel gave an anti-suicide message to kids entitled "You're Only Human." Tatiana and Johnny, a popular Latin American duo, sang "When We're Together," a song about teen chastity. Musicians around the world have rallied to raise money through benefit concerts for the poor, underprivileged, starving, and imprisoned.[2]

Although rock music can be used as a force for good, some of it is clearly anti-social and anti-life. Beamed into 23.5 million households through MTV, the pervading messages in many of the songs are life is cheap, violence is fun, and suicide is a solution. Taken together, the philosophies suggest a form of nihilism—a skepticism that says everything, including life, has no meaning or purpose. Although some of the following rock groups may be no longer popular, they provide a sampling of lyrics on three common themes in heavy metal music: suicide, sexual violence, and satanism.

Suicide Themes

In "Suicidal Failure," from the album *Suicidal Tendencies,* the songwriter claims that although he has no reasons, he just wants to die.[3]

Ozzy Osbourne says he doesn't advocate suicide, yet the lyrics to "Suicide Solution" talk about suicide as the only way to escape feelings of loneliness and psychological unrest.[4] Although Osbourne claims the song is really about alcohol (Suicide *Solution*), the lyrics have been blamed as contributing to the death of John McCollum, nineteen, who apparently committed suicide after listening to "Suicide Solution" for five hours. The McCollum family disagrees that the lyrics are about alcohol. The Institute for Bio-Acoustic Research found additional lyrics recorded in the soundtrack at a slower speed advising the listener to "Get a gun and try it. Shoot, shoot, shoot!" Another teenager, Steve Boucher, is reported to have shot himself in the head while listening to the song "Shoot to Thrill" by AC/DC.[5]

What kind of influence do lyrics like these have on teenage suicides? We don't know for sure, but it may be worse than most parents realize. In the last decade, the suicide rate in the 15- to 19-year-old bracket has gone up over 400 percent. In one year over 600,000 American teens attempted to take their lives. In the next 30 minutes in the USA, 29 teenagers will attempt suicide.

Sexual Violence Themes

As part of his act, Blackie Lawless, lead singer for the band WASP, wore a buzz saw blade between his legs and used it to attack a woman tied to a torture rack. He boasts, "We've tied women up on a rack during shows and pretended to cut their throats."[6]

Motley Crue, at one time one of the most popular groups with younger teenagers, recorded a song that talks about a man hating a woman and then killing her as he watches her face turning blue.[7]

On the cover of the album *Easy Prey,* a man is shown lying in wait as a girl in a bikini walks down the beach. On the back of the cover, the man is shown carrying the lifeless body of a woman over his shoulder. The lyrics talk about the need to satisfy lust and a crazed excitement resulting from the woman fighting back.[8] Neurotic perversions such as *sadism* (gratification from causing pain) and *masochism* (pleasure derived from self-suffering or humiliation) combine in this song to promote the "rape myth," the insane notion that women enjoy pain with sex and want to be forced to have sex.

Lizzy Borden, another heavy metal band, released a video that depicts the torture of a woman on stage. They lower her into a box marked "Lizzy's Toys" and bring an ax down, seemingly severing her head. While blood spews into the air, the lead singer smears it all over himself and then brings out what appears as a decapitated body for the audience to view.

The band's name comes from the story of Lizzy Borden, a little girl who killed her parents with eighty-one blows from an ax. According to the band's leader, "Lizzy," murder was the theme of their album, *Love You to Pieces.*[9]

Satanism Themes

Satanism (the worship of Satan) is on the rise, carrying with it stories of ritualistic killings, cemetery desecrations, and infant molestations. Bands like AC/DC have seemed to offer teenagers an invitation to join them on the "highway to hell." Other bands, such as Venom, Slayer, and Black Sabbath have offered "how-tos" on everything from virgin sacrifice to necrophilia (sex with the dead).

Professor Joe Stuessy, author of *The Heavy Metal User's Manual,* says that when the band Venom sings "Sacrifice," "the effect on some impressionable teens is that of a play-by-play prescription for a satanic ritual."[10] The lyrics talk about Lucifer as one's master and, under his influence, plunging a dagger into a woman's breast while demons rejoice at the sacrifice.[11] Dan Cuellar, a television reporter in San Antonio who has investigated several satanic crimes, believes that most teens don't know what satanic music is about. To them it may be just a fad, but says Cuellar, "The link we've found between kids and satanism is the music."[12] Cult expert Sandi Gallant of the San Francisco Police Department agrees, "No matter what heavy metal band leaders say, they are projecting an image to the kids that they are satanists. Children want to emulate the stars."[13]

* * * * *

Do themes like suicide, sexual violence, and satanism really affect our youth? Aren't the lyrics merely harmless fantasy and "fun"? As I was writing this chapter, a woman called to tell me about her son. At seventeen, Jim was respectful, achieving well in school, and attending church. Then he started running with the wrong crowd and began listening to AC/DC, Motley

Crue, and Iron Maiden. Within two weeks Jim's parents saw a tragic transformation of their son. Jim, who had loved and respected his sisters, scorned them and became rebellious. He started drinking and doing drugs. As a result he lost his self-esteem and the light in his eyes was gone. His parents said it was like living with a totally different person.

Nikki Sixx of the heavy metal band, Motley Crue, said in an interview: "The one thing I got from Hitler was the idea of the Nazi youth. I believe in the Motley youth. The youth of today are the leaders of tomorrow. They're young, they can be brainwashed and programmed."[14] Child psychologist David Elkind writes: "Clearly the most underestimated influence on young people today is the record business. Perhaps because most adults find the level of sound obnoxious, the harmonics jarring, and the lyrics incomprehensible, we prefer to ignore the impact of rock music on our offspring."[15]

Ignore it? We can't. The stakes are too high. We can't ignore the images, the words, the philosophies that can destroy the soul . . . and assume that our youth will not be touched by it.

What Parents Can Do:

• Listen to your teen's music. Gather information about their favorite singers and groups. Check out the lyrics in *Hit Parader* magazine or on the record jackets and read some of the literature on rock music. To be credible with our teens, we must know what we are talking about.

• Discuss rock music philosophy. Ask your teen what the lyrics mean. Because many teens think little about the *implications* of lyrics, don't assume they convey the same message that they do to you. If you feel the lyrics are harmful, tell your teen openly, firmly, and without anger or a judgmental attitude. Use your best listening and talking skills.

• Give your teen something better to believe in. This is a life-long process and is most fruitful when we begin before they are teens. It requires that we know what we believe, that our philosophy of life is adequate for life's demands, and that we act and talk in ways consistent with our deepest beliefs.

• Encourage a wide range of musical tastes. Treat your teen to the best in classical, choral, contemporary, and country music. Play the music you enjoy and talk about why you like it.

• Establish specific guidelines. What themes will you not allow to invade your home? Porno-rock? Songs and videos that glorify sexual promiscuity, violence, suicide, the occult, and drugs? Try to arrive at a clear understanding together rather than merely laying down the law. If a conflict arises over the guidelines, use the Conflict Resolution Model described in chapter ten.

DRUGS AND DRINKING

We live in a drug-taking, alcohol-consuming society and teenagers feel an enormous pressure to be part of it. The National Clearinghouse for Alcohol Information estimates that 450,000 persons under the age of twenty are already problem drinkers or alcoholics. A majority of junior high school students, and more than 90 percent of those in high school, have experimented with alcohol.

Awareness of what is happening in the teenage alcohol and drug culture is the first step toward taking preventive measures or solving existing problems. Here are facts we need to know.

Alcohol

—Alcohol-related highway deaths are the No. 1 killer of 15- to 24-year-olds. Over 50 percent of all highway fatalities in a given year are alcohol-related.

—In one study, 92.6 percent of high school seniors said they had tried alcohol; 39 percent reported participating in binge drinking, defined as five or more drinks in a row.

—Often underage drinkers are encouraged to drink by the ambivalence of parents about their own drinking habits.

—Legal drunkenness is not the only issue. Tests show that anyone who drinks is three to four times more likely to have an accident as one who does not drink.

Dick Dutton, director of Alcohol Education for Youth, Inc., and Brian Gleason, coordinator for the Teenage Alcoholism and Alcohol Abuse Rehabilitation Program, wrote the following in an article entitled, "It's Only Booze":

> A classic cartoon shows a teenager stretched out on a couch, "smashed," with eight or nine empty beer cans on the floor. His parents stand over him and the father says, "Thank God, it's only booze!" Parents have become so terrified of what they know so little about—pot, speed, cocaine and other drugs—that they have missed the increasingly devastating effect of alcohol.[16]

According to Dutton and Gleason, alcohol abuse is America's No. 1 drug problem. In most communities drinkers outnumber pot users by at least two to one, and for every heroin addict there are nearly forty-five alcoholics. For young people, alcohol is the drug of choice because of its availability, legality, and cultural acceptability.

Other Drugs

As we realize the extent of drug abuse in the USA and other countries of the world, solving the problem looks hopeless. Some authorities call the present drug situation an epidemic.

—Among youth between the ages of 12 and 17, one in three experimented with alcohol (illegal for this age group) and one in eight tried marijuana (also illegal) within the last month.

—Drug abuse costs us at least $100 billion annually in criminal activity, medical and legal services, and lost productivity.

—George Beschner, chief of the treatment research branch at the National Institute on Drug Abuse, estimates that multiple drug use has trapped as many as 1.2 million adolescents in America.

—When a Gallup Poll asked students thirteen to nineteen to identify the biggest problems currently confronting young people, drugs headed the list.

—Crack and wine coolers have taken the place of pot as top drugs tempting ten-year-olds. Crack is cocaine boiled down (it makes a cracking sound when heated) into crystalline balls that can be smoked. A gram of coke costs about $100, but two beads of crack go for $10.

—Every day 5000 teenagers and adults try cocaine for the first time. According to the National Institute on Drug Abuse, cocaine is a powerfully addictive drug which is dangerous in all forms.

—Youth almost never try cocaine, crack, or heroin without having first used such "gateway drugs" as tobacco, alcohol, and marijuana.

—According to Secretary of Education William J. Bennett, "Drug use impairs memory, alertness, and achievement. Drugs erode the capacity of students to perform in school, to think, and to act responsibly. The consequences of using drugs can last a lifetime."[17]

In a special report on America's war on drugs, *Time* editors wrote: "Fine white powder pours past the border patrol like sand through a sieve. On busy street corners and in urban parks, pushers murmur, 'Crack it up, crack it up,' like some kind of evil incantation, bewitching susceptible kids and threatening society's sense of order and security."[18]

Why would a potentially damaging and even life-threatening substance appeal to teenagers? Experts point to several deep-seated causes that produce a craving for drugs: lack of communication in the home, a sense of personal failure and despair, disintegration of the family, moral laxity, hedonism, and the relentless pressure to perform in a fast-paced society.

Part of the seductive power of drugs is their glamorization on TV with fast cars and fancy clothes and a society hooked on materialism. In one town, many parents were shocked when the body of a notorious local drug dealer, Felix Mitchell, was carried by a gold-and-black hearse, drawn by two bay horses, followed by a long line of Rolls-Royces and luxury cars. Inside the church where Mitchell lay in a bronze coffin with glittering rings on his fingers, a sound track played Sade's pop hit, "Smooth Operator." Although Mitchell, 32, had been stabbed to death while in Leavenworth penitentiary for a drug-trafficking conspiracy, *Time* reports that "in the faces of young people who lined the funeral route were expressions of awe."[19]

In a report to the nation by the President and Nancy Reagan, the First Lady stressed the vulnerability of the nation's youth: "Today there is a drug and alcohol epidemic in this country and no one is safe from it—not you, not me and certainly not our children, because this epidemic has *their* names written on it."[20]

What Parents Can Do:

• Listen. Listen to what your teen is saying about drugs in school. Listen for possible hints about experimenting with drugs.

• Learn the signs of drug use. Clinical psychologist Charles Hannaford suggests that parents note such symptoms in teens as:

—change in behavior toward being overly rebellious
—change in clothing style and image, doing more of the things identified with the drug culture
—change in musical taste, especially an interest in heavy metal music
—decrease in academic performance
—frequent outbursts of temper
—withdrawal and not spending time with the family
—being secretive about new friends.[21]

• Talk. Let it be known that drug use is not acceptable. Tell your teen why you hold that position. Be firm, clear, and direct. In one episode of "The Cosby Show," Dr. Clifford Huxtable (Cosby) told his son Theo: "You won't use drugs in this house. When you're eighteen and out on your own, you won't use drugs. When you're seventy-five and I'm dead, you still won't use drugs!"[22] When you talk, *speak the truth in love.* After *Time* magazine carried a cover story on drugs, a twelve-year-old boy wrote to the editor, "Many young people who run away or feel as if they are not loved turn to drugs. They think it's the only way out." We need to tell our teens and show them that it is not.

• Teach your teen how to say No. Role play with your teen the "broken record" technique (saying "no thanks" over and over) and the "cold shoulder" routine (simply ignoring the invitation). Help your teen or preteen to see resisting peer pressure ("come on, try it") as a sign of personal strength and victory.

• Take action. In *How to Get Your Child Off Marijuana,* the Menninger Foundation's Dr. Harold M. Voth advocates an aggressive approach to save a child from the consequences of smoking pot. He says that when a child is in danger and talking about the problem with him has failed, strong action is required. Dr. Voth advocates three principles for action that apply to other drugs as well as pot.

> The first principle is *intervention.* The key to saving your child from marijuana is to interpose yourself between him and the substance for at least three months. If your child denies using marijuana but your suspicions tell you otherwise, then you face a very difficult step: you must simply invade his privacy and carry out a thorough search of his living space and other areas, and do it more than once. Very few marijuana smokers can see what is happening to themselves. This fact explains why reason so rarely works as the method for getting someone to stop the practice.
>
> The second principle is *responsibility.* You, the parent, must temporarily assume responsibility for your child's life when he cannot adequately do so. Look your child squarely in the eye and tell him clearly and without the slightest equivocation that you are going to stop his use of marijuana.
>
> The third principle is *substitution.* Because the user of marijuana develops a craving for it, the parent must find a substitute that will satisfy the deeper needs in a child. The primary substitute should be the parent. Although some teens resist increased time with their parents, others welcome it and find that time for genuine dialogue meets their needs.[23]

• Read. The more you and I know, the more aware we become and better able to handle difficult situations. In a newspaper interview, the mother of a son who had become chemically dependent said: "I wish we'd known what to look for, the signs of chemical dependency. I wish I'd been more aware. I wish I'd known what the experts say about the connection between the lyrics of heavy metal music and the drug culture."[24] Check the resource section in the back of this book.

• Get professional help. If your son or daughter continues to take drugs and is not responding to your best efforts to deal with the situation, don't wait. Don't let pride get in your way. Don't deny the seriousness of the problem by saying, "He's just smoking pot; no big deal." or "She's going through a stage; it'll pass." First look for the best qualified counselor, clinical psychologist, or psychiatrist you can find. Then join a parents' support group.

• Fight to win. Face the fact that you are fighting a war . . . a war on drugs. Dr. Voth writes that parents need to commit themselves to this challenge with the degree of intensity men generate when they go into battle. *The enemy is not your teen, it's drugs.* Tell yourself victory can be the only outcome. When you save your child's life from drugs, everyone wins.

• Refuse to play the blame game. If you discover your teen is on drugs, you may experience feelings of guilt, hurt, anger, and helplessness. Rather than blaming your spouse ("You spoiled him!") or yourself ("I should have been more aware!") or your teen ("How could you do this to us?"), take immediate action that will help your teen solve the problem.

PREMARITAL SEX

A national poll of teenagers under seventeen revealed that more than half are sexually active, but only one-third of all parents talk to their children about sex.[25]

—According to one study, 3000 teenaged girls in America become pregnant each day. That's a million a year. Four out of five are unmarried. More than half get abortions. As *People* magazine reported, "They are babies having babies. Or killing them."[26]

—A Louis Harris poll indicated that 64 percent of the parents interviewed thought they had little or no control over their teenager's sexual activity and that they need outside help, primarily from the schools and through television.

—The word No has slipped from the family vocabulary. Parents don't teach their children to say No; teenagers don't realize they have a right to say No in the face of wrong.

—In response to a request by Ann Landers, 18,000 female readers wrote telling of the lines boyfriends use to pressure them into having sex:

"Come on. What are you afraid of? Don't be a baby. It's just part of growing up." "If you really loved me you would. That's the way people express their true feelings." "It's very painful for a guy to be in this condition and not get relief." "I want to marry you someday. We should find out if we are sexually compatible." "It will be good for your complexion."[27]

—While 10 percent of teenagers marry, the marriages tend to be short-lived. The divorce rate for parents younger than 18 is three times greater than that for parents who have their first child after age 20.[28]

—The AIDS virus has created a new urgency for responsible sex education. In a report on AIDS, U.S. Surgeon General C. Everett Koop stated, "There is no doubt that we need sex education in schools and that it must include information on heterosexual and homosexual relationships."[29]

Teenagers express a variety of views about their sexual activity. In an article on teenage fathers, fifteen-year-old Cliff had barely begun shaving when pregnancy flung him into parenthood unprepared financially and emotionally.

When my girlfriend told me she was pregnant, I wasn't really surprised. We'd been dating for two years and had been having sex a lot for the past eight months. Yeah, we talked about protection and sometimes I used condoms, but mostly we just liked having sex without even thinking about a baby. The night that she told me she'd missed her period, both of us got real scared . . . . We went to a doctor in the next town over and found out for sure she was pregnant.[30]

Seventeen-year-old Randy was vaguely aware that his sexual activity with his girlfriend could get her pregnant, but he was totally bewildered to discover that the birth of *her* child made him a *father.*

Oh, I knew about sex, but I didn't really believe what I knew. My younger brother knew that guns could kill people, but he really didn't believe it because his playmate fell down dead and then jumped up to play some more. I technically knew that sexual relations caused pregnancy, but I didn't actually believe it could happen to me. Looking back now, the act and the consequences were altogether separate in my mind. I was astonished when I learned that my sexual behavior had created life.[31]

Most teenage fathers don't understand that young babies take more than they give. When they find out how much time, money, attention, and patience are required of a parent, they often feel trapped. Groans Carl, 17:

If I'd only known how hard it was going to be, I'd never have let this happen. I thought only about the good times, teaching him to talk and to walk, feeding him every now and then. But he cries all the time, and I have to come up with so much money for his things I can't even afford records anymore! I hate my job, and feel like I'll never be able to finish high school.[32]

Teenage pregnancy costs. For the nation's taxpayers, it's $16 billion per year, but the human cost to hundreds of thousands of teenagers is beyond calculation. It would be difficult to overstate the tragedy in terms of unhappiness, lost opportunities, poverty, disease, lack of proper care of the children, and the guilt of the teenage parents.

Why do we have this problem? I believe there are three basic reasons. First, many teenagers don't know as much about the facts of life as we might think. One pregnant teenager said that her girlfriend told her that you can't get pregnant the first time you have sex. Unfortunately, teens learn what they know by rumor, on the streets, from firsthand experience, from friends (who have identical sources), or from media such as records, movies, and TV.

Second, teens face an almost constant barrage of distorted sexual imagery. The average teenager watches TV more than four hours daily—more time than they spend doing anything except going to school and sleeping. What do they see? Researchers reported that on prime-time network television, 20,000 sexual acts and innuendos took place in the course of a year. For four hours a day a teen lives in a world where no one ever says premarital sex is wrong, no one ever says No, no one ever gets pregnant, and where sexual relationships are often pictured as either recreational or violent.

Third, parents are not talking with their teens about sex. And they are not listening either. According to psychologist Sol Gordon of Syracuse University, surveys involving more than 8,000 students show that fewer than 15 percent reported that they received a meaningful sex education from their parents.[33] Our own survey shows that teens would like to talk with their parents about sexual matters, but they don't for three reasons:

1. They are afraid their parents will not know how to answer their questions.
2. They feel their parents will judge or make fun of them if they ask questions.
3. They think their parents will treat the subject too seriously.

What Parents Can Do:

• Talk. We need to start in early childhood, answering questions and supplying age-appropriate information in a relaxed and supportive manner. In addition to biological or physical facts, we must stress the importance of love, commitment, and permanence in marriage. We need to balance the media's messages with our own perspectives and deeply held beliefs. Spontaneous exchanges are best. Brief remarks on the part of parents allow more opportunities for teens to continue the discussion. The most effective talk results when we put ourselves in our teen's situation and think, "*How* would I want my parent to talk to me about sex?"

• Listen. We need to listen in such a way that our teens will feel their questions are important to us and that we will not jump to conclusions about their sexual activity if they ask questions that are explicit. If a daughter asks, "When a girl misses taking one birth control pill, can she get pregnant?" we must not assume that the daughter is taking birth control pills or anxiously ask, "Are you pregnant?" That kind of response could make the daughter feel that the parent doesn't trust her and drive her to the very behavior we fear. She might reason, "Since my mother suspects that I am having sex, I might as well."

• Build personal responsibility. Since we can't be with our teens every minute, we can't control their sexual activity; however, we can teach that premarital sex is wrong. We can build a sense of responsibility for their own bodies. We can help them to look into the future, as hard as that may be for teens, and set some goals for the kind of life and relationships they want to develop. Some TV programs and movies present excellent teaching opportunities when, beneath all the glamour and glitter, they show the tragic results and deep unhappiness resulting from premarital or extramarital sex.

• Teach "Just Say No!" When ABC *Nightline* moderator, Ted Koppel, gave a commencement address at Duke University, he declared:

> We have actually convinced ourselves that slogans will save us . . . . Enjoy sex whenever and with whomever you wish, but wear a condom. No! The answer is No. Not because it isn't cool or smart or because you might end up in jail or dying in an AIDS ward, but No because it's wrong . . . . In its purest form, truth is not a polite tap on the shoulder. It is a howling reproach. What Moses brought down from Mount Sinai were not the Ten Suggestions.[34]

Let us teach that saying No to wrong is saying Yes to victory. Let us teach that our teens may need to say No not only to the one they are dating, but also to their own feelings and passions. Let us teach that saying No is a sign of courage, of marching to the beat of a different drummer, of belonging to the Kingdom of God. When they know *why* to say No, we can better teach them *how* to say No.

— No. If you really loved me you wouldn't ask.
— I have decided no sex before marriage—so don't pressure me.
— I don't care if "everyone's doing it." Sex is not for me until marriage.
— I respect your feelings and I ask you to respect mine. The answer is No.

— If my No makes you go, then that proves I am only a
sex object to you. The answer is No.

— Yes I love you, but I believe a sexual relationship is to
be reserved for marriage. My self-respect is too important to settle for second best. If you can't accept my
No, that is your problem.

— I know that No now means Yes to a future of self-
respect.

• Get the facts straight. Good books on the subject of
talking to teenagers about sex are available (see the resource
section). It is our responsibility to prepare on this most important subject as well as possible . . . to prepare at least as well
as one would for a speech to the PTA or civic group. Talking to
our teens with clarity of purpose and giving accurate information can enable them to disregard misinformation they will
receive from others.

• Teach the beauty of sex. In their fear of premarital sex,
some parents try to tell their teens that sex is dirty and dangerous. But we need to teach that sex is one of God's great gifts to
us and that within the context of marriage, it is enjoyable, satisfying, fulfilling. Teach them that their sexuality is *intended* by
God and viewed by him as *good:* "So God created man in his
own image, in the image of God he created him; male and
female he created them . . . . God saw all that he had made,
and it was very good" (Genesis 1:27, 31).

• Teach that marriage is ordained by God: "For this reason a man will leave his father and mother and be united to his
wife, and they will become one flesh. The man and his wife
were both naked, and they felt no shame" (Genesis 2:24, 25).

• Teach the jubilation of romance and marriage in the
Song of Solomon.

Lover
How beautiful you are, my darling!
　　Oh how beautiful!
　　Your eyes are doves. (1:15)
Beloved
How handsome you are, my lover!
　　Oh, how charming!
　　And our bed is verdant. (1:16)

• Teach that premarital sex is a sin against one's body and dishonors God: "Flee from sexual immorality. All other sins (one) commits are outside his body, but he who sins sexually sins against his own body. Do you know that your body is a temple of the Holy Spirit, who is in you, whom you have received from God? You are not your own; you were bought at a price. Therefore honor God with your body" (1 Corinthians 6:18–20).

• Express your love to your teenager daily. Teens need to know you love them or they will look for love in the wrong places. Premarital sex among teenagers is often not a problem of the intellect, but a problem of the feelings. Some feel a tremendous urge to trade their bodies for love and acceptance. The thesis is this: Passions are more subject to control when teens' basic emotional needs for love, acceptance, and security are being met by their parents.

• Practice forgiveness. If teens go too far, they need correction and reproof, yes, but they also need to rebuild their lives. Encourage them to confess their sin before God and then to receive his forgiveness. Help them to see that whenever we sincerely pray the Lord's Prayer, we acknowledge that we all have sinned (Forgive us our sins) and we promise the Lord we will forgive others (as we forgive those who have sinned against us), regardless of how much hurt they may have caused us. Forgiveness is communicated best by saying the actual words "I forgive you" and showing acceptance and love *in ways that are meaningful to the teen* (tone of voice, facial expression, kindness, hugs, willingness to listen).

• Build upon your relational power. In *How to Help Your Child Say "No" to Sexual Pressure,* Josh McDowell writes:

> If I were asked to give the number-one contributing factor to the adolescent sexuality crisis, at the top of my list would be adolescent alienation brought on by parental inattentiveness. If you want to insulate your child from the many sexual pressures, develop a close, open relationship of mutual respect and love. Establishing sexual prohibitions and rules without a relationship often leads to rebellion. But rules within the context of a loving parent relationship generally lead to a positive response.[35]

• Explain the reasons for chastity. First, God requires it. Chastity is his will for our wholeness. Second, abstinence from sex until marriage is part of God's law because it keeps us free:

> free from guilt and loss of fellowship with God
> free from pregnancy and venereal disease
> free from having to choose a hurry-up wedding
> free from loss of self-respect and reputation
> free from exploitation by others
> free to expand options for personal development
> free to sublimate sexual energy for growth in other areas
> free to develop many healthy relationships
> free to feel good about ourselves
> free to enjoy God's favor and serve him with enthusiasm.

*   *   *   *

Newspapers provide plenty of opportunity for talking about our values in life. One night a few years ago, I read a review of a movie described as "raucously funny" in which a man wanted to kill his wife, but before he could carry out his scheme, she was kidnapped . . . to his great relief and amusement. In the same paper there was a news account of a man who killed his wife, two children, and then himself. We talked about the fact that there is a pervasive evil in much of our society that produces a desperate unhappiness, and that some try to cover up the despair or meaninglessness with a sick form of humor, such as the movie that was advertised. Then I said,

> Children, Mom and I want to assure you that our philosophy of life and our experience in relationships is quite different from that in a large part of our society. Our goal is for you to experience life in all of its fullness. We want you to have a healthy self-esteem so that you will not allow yourselves to be manipulated or intimidated by anyone. There is nothing funny about hate and revenge and hurting others. Some people laugh at evil in human relationships because they think that is their only alternative. It isn't. We know that forgiveness, meaning, and purpose are available to anyone through faith in Jesus Christ.

TEEN SUICIDE

Suicide is the ultimate withdrawal from relationship. It is a tragic message, a struggle to get in the last word. In a guest editorial in *USA Today,* Richard Krawiec wrote: "Suicide is a desperate scream, a final attempt to communicate how [teenagers] feel about life and the world they inhabit."[36]

Because of its terrible finality, no parent can get used to reports like the following:

> ALSIP, ILL. (AP)—Two young women, one holding a rose and a stuffed animal, the other a photo album, were found dead in a garage, apparently victims of the same method of suicide used by four teenagers in New Jersey, police said yesterday.[37]

Parents, stunned by the recent rise in teen suicide, realize they cannot arrogantly assume "That will never happen to my child."

—Every hour, on the average, someone in the United States 24 years old or younger commits suicide.[38]

—Suicide ranks as the third most common teen killer behind accidents and homicides, and some experts think a good number of accidents may actually be suicides.[39]

—73 percent of the 500 teenagers who responded to a *TeenAge* magazine survey said they have thought about committing suicide and 70 percent said they knew someone who attempted suicide.[40]

—The reason most often given for contemplating suicide was "not getting along with parents," followed by a fear of not being able to live up to other people's expectations. Loneliness, boyfriend problems, and concern about appearance were also mentioned as major reasons.[41]

—About a quarter of the teens in this survey said that they have no one to whom they can talk about their suicidal thoughts; 15 percent said they don't think their problems are important enough to talk about.[42]

Dr. R. John Kinkel, who reported on teen suicide to the American Psychiatric Association, said that people have underestimated the prevalence of teen suicide. Nearly eight of 100

U.S. teenagers attempt suicide every year, more than experts had previously believed. The results of his study of nearly 3,000 adolescents (the largest ever done on the subject in the U.S.) closely links drug and alcohol use with suicide attempts. He also found that suicide attempts were twice as common among females, with the most vulnerable being between the ages of 14 and 16.[43]

What causes a teen to attempt suicide? In addition to drugs and alcohol, experts think contributing factors include sexual involvement, family crisis, depression, loneliness, rejection, lack of communication, poor self-image, unrelieved stress, and a feeling of not meeting expectations and standards. Sometimes there are no apparent answers—only questions.

Often words, behavior, and circumstances are clues that can alert parents to the possibility of a teen's suicidal tendencies. Word clues include statements such as "I might as well kill myself," or "I suppose you would be happier if I weren't around anymore," or "Nothing matters; it's no use." Behavioral clues might include prolonged depression, signs of despair, disorientation, and panic or acts of self-destruction through alcoholism, drug abuse, or reckless driving. We should also consider such stressful events as the divorce of parents, failing a final exam, being rejected by a girlfriend/boyfriend, and the death of a parent, grandparent, friend, or pet as possible high risk times.

When these or other clues alert us to the fact that something is very wrong, what can we do? What can we say? Parents often do and say nothing because they don't want to make matters worse and they have no clear idea of what to do.

What Parents Can Do:

• Get help. If you suspect that your teenager may be suicidal, don't delay in contacting a qualified counselor or psychologist.

• Listen hard. Force yourself to not comment on or contradict every negative statement. If your teen says, "Life is meaningless!", don't say "Oh no it's not! That's a terrible thing to say!" Instead say, "Life looks pretty awful to you right now" and then listen. The goal is to keep the channels of communication open. If teenagers vent feelings through talking, they will often feel some relief from stress. Parents release an awesome healing power when they choose deep and active listening.

• Take the initiative. A depressed teenager may want to talk, but not know how to begin. Don't be afraid to be direct. "I've noticed that you seem troubled lately. Let's talk about it. I'm ready to listen." Come right out and ask, "Are you happy?" If your teen says "No," do your best to find out why.

• Demonstrate love. Even when our teens seem to be doing everything to incur our wrath, we need to convey unconditional positive regard for them as persons. We must never let them think that some failure or embarrassment that they may have brought upon the family will lead to the loss of our love.

• Write messages to your teenager. Talking face to face about problems can be very difficult, especially when emotions run high. We may communicate much better by taking the time to think through what we really want to say and writing it down. As we read what we have written, we can ask ourselves, "Is this what I really want to say? Is it fair? Does it convey not only my concern or disagreement, but also my love and support?"

• Teach coping skills. As a long-term preventive measure, we need to talk with our teens about how we have learned to handle the bumps and bruises of everyday life. Many teens have tunnel vision. They need help in seeing a broader view. At the dinner table one night, I tried to do this by telling the children what happened when my girlfriend in college broke up with me. I told them that at the time I felt it was the worst thing that had ever happened to me. We laughed as I told them how I kicked a telephone pole in my anger and then hopped around in pain . . . how injury was added to insult. I explained that now I am very glad that event occurred in my life for I believe that in the breakup of that relationship, God was preparing me for one who would be much better suited for me—their mother.

• Use networking. Most families cannot survive the destructive pressures from all parts of society without the help of friends who care and are willing to be mutually supportive.

In the ups and downs of parenting, my family has gained tremendous support and long-term positive influence from youth advisors, teachers, adult role models, and our children's peers who were committed to similar values.

• Talk about options. Suicide occurs because young people feel that is their only option. We must help them to see—not just by words, but by our lives—that life is worth living, that there is more than one way to deal with problems, that we will work at solving problems with them, that we really are on their team. We must help them to realize that the mood swings and depressive fits of adolescence are survivable, that mistakes and failures are not measures of one's worth, and that the great part of being a human being is the capacity to choose a new beginning with the help of God.

* * * * *

If you are suffering because your teen has made some wrong choices, don't panic. Go to a pastor, counselor, or friend with whom you can be completely honest, and unburden your heart. Go also to God in prayer.

> O God, my heart is heavy. I'm emotionally drained, frustrated, and angry. I don't know where to turn or what to do. Why should this happen to me? I've tried so hard to be a good parent, but now I feel like a total failure. Where did I go wrong?
> Heavenly Father, help me. Clear my mind and cleanse my heart. Give me the wisdom and inner strength I need to deal with this situation. Enable me to express the right kind of love and firmness. May I listen with compassion and talk with conviction.
> Grant that I may have the serenity to accept what cannot be changed, the courage to change what can be changed, and the wisdom to know the one from the other.[44]
>
> Amen.

ACTION STEPS FOR POSITIVE COMMUNICATION

1. When you listen to your teen's music, what are the themes you detect? In the "Rock Music Philosophies" section, several steps are recommended for parents. Using them as a

springboard for your own ideas, what approach to your teen's music will you take?

2. What kind of action on your part would head off a problem with drinking and drugs? Write out the messages you want to get across to your teen on this subject.

3. List the key concepts you feel your teen should know about sex. Determine how and when you plan to discuss them with your teen.

4. How can you help your teen to love and enjoy life and thereby decrease the chances of your teen even contemplating suicide?

It's hard to rebel when I know you're trying to understand.

Tim, 15, to his mother

 10

Resolving Conflict

In recent seminars I have asked parents to jot down how they responded to their teenagers during their last major conflict. Here are some of the typical responses:

—I lost my head and said some mean things.
—I cried.
—I made some irrational demands and grounded my son for a month.
—I slapped my daughter across the face.
—With one word I blew a relationship I had spent years building.

Most parents want to respond differently. We want alternatives to giving in or getting even. This chapter provides a model for resolving conflict that works even when the heat is on.

GETTING A GRIP ON CONFLICT

Before we can use the Conflict Resolution (CR) Model effectively, we need to get a mental grip on the nature of the conflict. As a way of stimulating thinking on this matter, check whether you agree or disagree with the following statements.[1]

Your Opinion on Conflict

Agree Disagree

_____ _____ 1. It is sometimes necessary to yell at our teens to get them to do what we want.

_____ _____ 2. We must compromise our convictions to maintain peace in the home.

_____ _____ 3. Negotiation is to be reserved for adults, not teenagers.

_____ _____ 4. If we admit mistakes to our teens, we will lose our authority over them and their respect.

_____ _____ 5. It is better to give in to our teens than to refuse their wishes and make them angry with us.

_____ _____ 6. The Bible teaches that it's wrong to get angry.

_____ _____ 7. It is better to say whatever comes into our minds than to follow a plan or model for resolving conflict.

Resolving conflicts *does* require us to make careful distinctions. For example, although disagreements between parents and teens are inevitable, it is not true that yelling, hitting, or name-calling are also inevitable. In fact, this chapter is built on the conviction that such fights can be avoided and conflicts can be resolved calmly.

It is helpful to remember that these conflicts have a healthy side. They are part of growing up. In *Try Being a Teenager,* Earl Wilson charts conflict as an expected result of a collision between the adolescent's desire for freedom and the parent's need for control.[2]

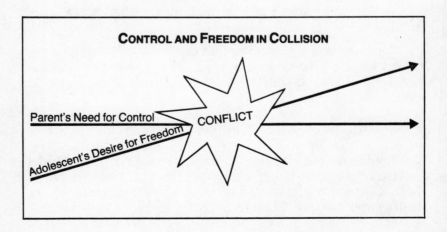
CONTROL AND FREEDOM IN COLLISION

Parent's Need for Control

Adolescent's Desire for Freedom

CONFLICT

David Augsburger, in *Caring Enough to Confront,* writes, "Conflict is natural, normal, neutral, and sometimes even delightful. It can turn into painful or disastrous ends, but it doesn't need to. Conflict is neither good nor bad, right nor wrong. Conflict simply is. How we view, approach and work through our differences does—to a large extent—determine our whole life pattern."[3] These thoughts give us hope. They allow us to look at resolving conflict with more objectivity. They reduce the fear and defensiveness we often have about conflict, because they suggest that conflicts with our teens are not always our fault after all . . . or theirs!

If we are to get a grip on conflict we will need to do two things. First, *accept temporary conflict as normal.* We need to make an allowance for it in our minds and in our relationships with our teens. In fact, we need to expect it, anticipate it, prepare for it. Second, we need to *follow a model for conflict resolution* that shows us the steps to take. Knowing where we are headed will enable us to relax a bit. We can channel what we think and feel in a positive direction. The first step involves adjusting our attitude; the second requires learning a skill. When we master both, conflict becomes manageable.

THE WINNING OPTION

Conflicts that degenerate into sharp words and hurt feelings can burn their way into our memories and provoke two common responses: *retreat* and *revenge.* When we retreat, we suppress our feelings, flare up in other contexts, and make ourselves and others miserable. When we try revenge, we set in motion a lose-lose situation of blame and counterblame.

> Why pick on me? What did I do?
> It's not my fault—it's yours.
> Why did you get us into such a mess?
> You made me do it!
> How stupid can you get?

The Apostle James wrote that the tongue is small, like a spark, but it can set a whole forest aflame.[4] Both retreat and revenge escalate the blaze out of control. Instead of restoring relationship, they intensify the conflict. No one wins.

The winning option is *resolution*—talking through a conflict and quenching the fire of discord. We choose a tone of voice that conveys respect even when we're upset. We do not repress feelings or engage in cover-up, do not automatically assume all blame or try to fix all blame. Rather, we recognize that any number of factors can contribute to conflict. Among them are

— psychological stress
— wrong assumptions
— poor communication
— frustrated plans
— unrealized dreams
— poor self-image
— hormonal imbalance
— misunderstanding
— fatigue
— rejection
— too much pressure
— feelings of failure.

Whatever the causes of conflict, we can choose the winning option and follow a plan that will enable us to stop falling into the same old arguments.

A MODEL FOR CONFLICT RESOLUTION

In the heat of an argument, we don't think as clearly as we might. That's why we need a model, a pattern to follow that guides us toward our goal. The following model helps us program our minds so that in the midst of a conflict, what comes out of our mouths is not destructive, but constructive. For the model to work we must take four steps that lead to resolving conflicts and develop the communicating skills to carry them out.[5]

	Steps	Messages
1.	Define the problem.	("I hear . . .")
2.	Look for agreement.	("I agree . . .")

3. Understand feelings.   ("I understand . . .")
4. State views calmly.   ("I think . . .")

Especially during those times of impasse, when neither we nor our teenagers seem to make any sense to the other, we will find this Conflict Resolution (CR) Model useful. At first it may seem unnatural and mechanical—like learning to ride a bike for the first time—but with practice this model can become second nature. It will help us maintain balance and become adept at talking through conflicts to their resolution.

The first step is to *define the problem.* In any given conflict, do we really know what the problem is or are we misjudging the motive and the intent of our teenagers? Are we making wrong assumptions about what they are trying to communicate?

When the real problem is not defined, mistaken assumptions proliferate and relationships deteriorate. Our teens may say one thing and we believe them to have said something quite different and argue against what we believe they said. Our teens, not understanding our objections (which may be quite legitimate objections to what our teens *didn't* say), then defend their original statement with further argument. These additional arguments, interpreted in light of our mistaken assumptions, lead to further mistaken assumptions on our part, which in turn thoroughly confuse and anger our teens. In a matter of seconds, the argument can be hundreds of miles away from the real problem.

In the latter stages of writing this book with my son, we faced the pressure of much to do and little time in which to do it. I remember one night when the pressure, combined with wrong assumptions, contributed to a major conflict between us. I complained that Jud was procrastinating. He countered with evidence that proved to him that he was working as hard as he could. Further, he felt hurt because he thought that I was questioning his commitment to our project. I was unhappy because he was angry at me for trying to help. The conflict began to be resolved when we worked on defining the problem. It became clear to both of us that the problem was not Jud's procrastination, as I had assumed, or my questioning his commitment, as Jud had thought. When we defined the real problem *behind* the conflict—Jud's uncertainty about how to proceed—we took the biggest step toward resolving the conflict.

To avoid mistaken assumptions, we can begin to define the problem by saying one of the following:

— I hear you saying that . . .
— Are you saying that . . . ?
— What really is our problem?
— It seems to me that the problem is . . . . Right?

Refuse to consider new material until you both agree on the problem.

Second, *look for agreement*. Normally we will find several points in our teens' arguments with which we can agree . . . if we *listen* for them. When we acknowledge areas of agreement, we limit the scope of the argument, thus making seemingly overwhelming problems more manageable. This in turn reduces tension and turns the problem-solving process in a positive direction.

To express areas of agreement, say "I agree that . . ." and then focus on details on which you both can honestly agree.

— I agree that I said some harsh words to you. I'm sorry.
— I agree that you tried to get home on time.
— I agree that many of your friends are dating already.
— I agree that the movie is rated PG-13 and you are 14.

To find areas of agreement requires active listening on our part—and that is part of its strength. One of the most frequent complaints we hear from teenagers is that parents don't listen to them . . . especially when an issue looms between them. Although our teens usually know that they can't get their way on every issue, they do expect us to listen. When they know we have listened enough to recognize where we and they agree, we send a powerful message of respect.

Third, *understand feelings*. Few things are more important to our teens than their feelings. If we misunderstand their feelings, we will not be heard when we try to make our points.

By taking time to understand feelings, we convey respect for what to them is the most dominant part of them as persons. If genuine understanding of their feelings is what they really want, the conflict may be resolved at this point and a psychological closeness restored.

Caution! Do not say, "I understand exactly how you feel." The classic response is, "Oh no you don't!" Instead, say, "I understand that you *might* feel . . ." and then complete the sentence with one word describing the feeling. What seems like a small difference between these two messages really is a big one. The first conveys to our teens that we are making too many unwarranted assumptions about how they feel. It's almost always offensive. The second message tells them that we genuinely want to understand and will take time to find out how they really feel.

Another caution: Don't try *too* hard to understand, because sometimes teens do not really understand their own feelings or they may not want us to know exactly how they feel. If we are not sensitive at this point, we could end up embarrassing them for not knowing how to explain their feelings . . . or angering them because we are prying into their secret domain. Yet, the benefits of understanding feelings are worth some risks if we proceed with sensitivity.

Try to complete the sentence "I understand that you might feel . . ." with one word that accurately describes the feeling your teen communicated to you. You might use one of the following:

angry	troubled
defensive	upset
depressed	uncertain
hurt	revengeful
worried	elated
anxious	happy
afraid	confident

Always convey this message with the impression that you are willing to be corrected if wrong. "I understand that you might feel . . . . Right?" Tendering our perceptions encourages them to correct us when we are wrong. When we state the feeling accurately, we take one more giant step toward resolving the conflict.

Fourth, *state your views calmly.* Begin by saying, "I think . . ." or "The way I see it, . . ." and then calmly and briefly state your opinion. The objective here is to help teens see our point of view as well as their own, and to persuade them to work with us in solving the problem.

—I think that our getting-off-to-school routine is not working. Somehow we have to stop the yelling and last-minute panic. Neither of us likes it when the other is angry. If we start breakfast at 6:30 A.M., we can make it without undue pressure.

—The way I see it, you're not getting the sleep you need. When one feels exhausted, everything suffers: health, personality, grades. Nothing seems to go right. I think it is reasonable to ask you to be in bed by 11:00 P.M. on school nights.

—Son, I want us to solve this problem together. I would like to give you an opportunity to suggest options that would be acceptable to us both.

Notice the emphasis on calmness. If calmness is not your normal reaction to discord and stress, you will have to work extra hard to establish a new pattern, but it can be done. Decide whether the old pattern of yelling and screaming is working. Is it drawing you and your teen together or forcing you apart? Does it help achieve understanding or destroy it? Does it teach your teen how to deal effectively with interpersonal conflict or does it merely make you feel better because you ventilated your feelings?

In discussing this chapter with my son, Jud said, "Dad, do you know why I don't yell and scream at you? It's because I don't need to. I know you will listen and try to be fair in your response." I'm grateful Jud feels that way because I hate discord. I won't allow constant friction in our home. Life is too short and relationships are too important. Neither retreat nor revenge solves problems. They smolder and flare up again later. When I use this CR Model, it provides me with the structure I need to handle the petty aggravations as well as the potentially explosive problems. I choose to speak firmly, without raising my voice, and I choose not to threaten. Although threats might give me a temporary upperhand, they rarely win the victory I seek.

* * * * *

When we choose to resolve conflict, we will notice a change in the focus of our conversations. The direction of the controversy begins to change from attacking each other to attacking a mutual problem and solving it. We can diagram the shift this way:

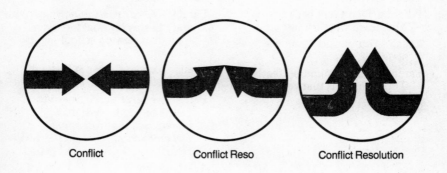

Conflict   Conflict Reso   Conflict Resolution

As the shift in focus occurs, we experience a corresponding change in the quality of our communicating.

1. We will speak *with*, not *at*, our teens.
2. We will be less defensive and more open.
3. We will be less angry and achieve greater understanding.

RESOLVING COMMON CONFLICTS

In this section, we will apply the four-step Conflict Resolution (CR) Model to common conflicts between parents and teenagers and compare the "discord exchange" (the way conflicts often develop when we have no plan) with the "resolution exchange" (which follows the CR Model). Each problem area begins with a conflict-producing statement. Although the dialogues are necessarily condensed, we will likely sense parallels to our experiences.

Problem Area: Curfew

Teenager, 15: I'll be late getting home tonight. The guys are having a party at Jack's house after the game.

Discord Exchange	Resolution Exchange
Parent: Not tonight. You have to be home by 11:00.	Parent: What do you mean by late?
Teen: No way!	Teen: About 1:00.
Parent: Don't talk back to me! You heard what I said!	Parent: *I hear you saying* you want to stay out that late even though curfew on school nights is 11:00.
Teen: You just don't understand!	Teen: I know, Dad, but I hate to be the first one to leave.
Parent: I understand perfectly! The problem is that you never listen!	Parent: I *agree* that it's hard to be the one to leave first. *I understand that you might feel embarrassed . . . right?*
etc.	Teen: Right.
	Parent: *I think that* we need to remember that you've gotten to sleep late the past few nights and you've complained about being very tired. I know it will be tough, but I'd like you to be home by 11:00.

Comment: Our natural tendency to follow the "Discord Exchange" is understandable, especially when we feel tired and we've heard the same tune before, but it doesn't go anywhere. No real understanding results and the cycle of mutual recriminations is likely to continue. The "Resolution Exchange" uncovered a feeling which might seem inconsequential from a parent's point of view, but it is important to the teen. The approach of understanding feelings combined with firmness to a standard is likely to produce in our teens a willingness to cooperate.

Problem Area: Chores

Teenage, 13:   I'm going to Judy's house to listen to some records!

Discord Exchange

Parent: Have you done your chores? (with a negative tone of voice)

Teen: I just did!

Parent: Then please fold your clothes.

Teen: Mom, I have plans!

Parent: You can take five minutes to do that for me.

Teen: No! (muttered)

Parent: Go to your room!

Teen: (leaves, slamming door)

Resolution Exchange

Parent: Have you done your chores? (with a positive tone of voice)

Teen: What chores?

Parent: The ones we discussed this morning.

Teen: Well, some of them.

Parent: *I heard* you saying that you want to go to Judy's, but you haven't completed your chores as we agreed.

Teen: But it's getting late and if I don't go now there won't be any time left.

Parent: *I agree* that time is a factor. *I understand that you might feel* frustrated by so much to do and so little time to do it. *Right?*

Teen: Very!

Parent: *I think* that if you had started sooner you would have been finished now. True?

Teen: I guess so.

Parent: What you agreed to do will not take long if you hop to it. Let's get it done.

Teen: OK, Mom.

Comment: The "Discord Exchange" is taken from an actual dialogue a thirteen-year-old girl wrote on one of our surveys. She feels she has a very good relationship with her parents and says that one message she most wants to communicate to them is that she loves them. But she complains that the biggest mistake parents make is not really listening to their kids. The "Resolution Exchange" may take more time and more thought, but the effort is likely to provide more opportunities for our teens to convey the messages they most want to give us.

Problem Area: Dating

> Teenager, 14: Mom, Brad asked me to go to a movie with him. I want to go.

Discord Exchange	Resolution Exchange
Parent: Absolutely not. Brad is a creep!	Parent: *I hear* you saying that you want to go out with a boy we discussed before.
Teen: He is not! All the girls go wild over him.	Teen: I know, Mom, but this is a chance in a lifetime.
Parent: He's not your type.	Parent: *I agree* that his picture is handsome.
Teen: Yes he is! I like him!	Teen: All the girls are crazy about him.
Parent: But I don't! That's final!	Parent: *I understand that you might feel* excited about this opportunity.
Teen: Who asked you? I'm going to run my own life!	Teen: Yes, I am!
etc.	Parent: *I think* that no matter how nice he looks, we need to hold to our plan for dating. Let's review the plan.

Comment: This "Resolution Exchange" will not be easy. The conflict may continue for some time, but the strength of this exchange is that the parent and teen are still talking. When the communication channels remain open, real life training can occur.

Problem Area: Music

Teenager, 17:   (playing loud rock music)

Discord Exchange	*Resolution Exchange*
Parent: I hate that music! Turn it off.	Parent: Tom, *I hear* some lyrics that are unacceptable.
Teen: I like it!	Teen: I don't listen to the lyrics. I just like the sound.
Parent: I heard it's devilish.	
Teen: It's harmless! Everybody listens to it!	Parent: *I agree* that this group has a sound that most teenagers would like.
Parent: I don't want you to listen to it!	Teen: It makes me feel good.
Teen: Why not?	Parent: *I understand that you might feel* happy when you hear that sound. But *I'm more concerned* about what might be getting into your head without your knowing it. Let's listen to the lyrics together and I'll point out what I mean.
Parent: Turn it off!	

Comment: At seventeen years of age the balance of power for determining the direction of life has already swung over to the teenager. If we engage a teenager in a power struggle, we will likely lose, yet the time for providing influence and direction is not over. Older teens are more capable of reasoning things out. While they are very much aware of their need for independence, they also want to know what we think and why we think as we do. If we can share ourselves with them in a winsome way and reduce the sense that we are dictating what they should do, we will gain a hearing.

* * * * *

No plan can guarantee peace, but a plan for resolving conflicts peacefully is definitely more promising than no plan. As we become familiar with the Conflict Resolution (CR) Model, it can be a powerful guide for what we say and how we say it. We may not always use the words "I hear," "I agree," "I understand," or "I think" or always take all these steps in every conflict. Conversations and conflicts don't usually follow such neat structures. Yet, the CR Model can guide us into the habit of resolving conflict using some or all of these steps.

1. Define the problem
2. Look for agreement
3. Understand feelings
4. State views calmly.

The following chart summarizes what to avoid and what to aim for when we face conflict.[6]

Discord/Resolution Chart

DISCORD PRODUCER	CONFLICT RESOLVER
1. Immediately assumes he knows what the problem is	1. Takes the time to discover and define the real problem
2. Tries to gain upper hand and prove his correctness	2. Looks for areas of agreement to reduce threat and signal a desire to resolve the conflict
3. Talks—doesn't listen	3. Listens actively to understand how the other person feels
4. Allows choices and actions to be dominated by feelings	4. States his viewpoints calmly, but firmly

With practice, the CR Model can become part of our communicating style and distinguish us from those who produce and experience the pain of continuing discord with their teenagers.

ACTION STEPS FOR POSITIVE COMMUNICATION

1. Review your answers in the section "Your Opinion on Conflict." After reading this chapter, would you still answer the same way?

2. In the section "The Winning Option," three responses to conflict were discussed: retreat, revenge, and resolution. If you are committed to a resolution response, what steps are you ready to take to make it a winning option for you?

3. Describe an unresolved conflict you have had with your teenager. The conflict was about _____ and has continued because _____.

4. Write out a "Resolution Exchange" as you imagine it would develop if you used the CR Model expressions "I hear . . . ," "I agree . . . ," "I understand that you might feel . . . ," and "I think. . . ."

Resolution Exchange

Parent/Teen Conflict

_____

_____

Parent: I hear _____

_____

Teen: _____

_____

Parent: I agree _____

_____

Teen: _____

_____

Parent: I understand that you might feel _____.
Right?

Teen: _____

_____

Parent: I think _____

_____

> My parents had given me everything
> they could possibly owe a child and
> more. Now it was my turn to decide
> and nobody . . . could help me very
> far. . . ."[1]

Novelist Graham Green

Talking about Life's Major Decisions

With so many questions to be answered and so many choices to be made, our teens find the last years of high school a critical time. These decisions are theirs, not ours. Graham Green was right . . . we can't help them "very far," but we can help them ask the right questions and walk a few steps with them through their confusion toward their highest goals.

It's not easy to lead them even a few steps. They have a built-in need to carve out their identity, to choose their path, to become their own person. Since too much direction on our part disrupts their drive for independence, we need to prepare carefully for those strategic moments when they want to talk and need to hear the best help we can give them.

To do this with confidence, we need to know *what we value most*. We cannot transfer to our teens what is unclear in our own minds. I have learned that the values upon which I have built my life are not easily shared. Is that true for you? Perhaps the reason is that we did our foundational thinking years ago and, as adults, have focused our day-to-day attention on building upon that foundation. It may have been years since we really examined the foundation for what we think and do. When we clarify that foundation in our minds, we are ready to take the next step.

Second, we need to know *how to talk about what we value most*. We will have to muster all the communication skills we have learned thus far to win a hearing. Of course, it's worth the effort. The successful transfer of significant values is the rewarding part of parenting. It's rounding the far turn and heading into the homestretch. It's seeing all the seeds that have been planted from day one beginning to blossom. It's hearing our teens say, "Thanks, Mom. That means a lot to me." "Thanks, Dad. That's just what I needed to hear."

In this chapter, we will review values I believe are foundational in five major decision areas:

1. Education
2. Vocation
3. Money
4. Marriage
5. Faith

To communicate what we believe in these areas, I suggest a three-step process: ponder facts, transfer values, and practice some "door-openers."

EDUCATION: WHAT DO I WANT TO KNOW?

The summer before his senior year, my son Jud received a host of brochures in the mail each advertising a particular college or field of study. If your daughter or son is at this decision stage, you know the immensity of the concerns. You may hear statements that punctuate the anxiety your teen feels:

This is a big deal. I really am growing up. I'm going to have to decide what I want to do with my life. What training do I want? Where can I get it? Do I want to go to college? Will I be accepted? Can I afford it? What happens if I fail? Help!

Points to Ponder about Education

• Children have different learning and maturity rates. Our school systems are based on the chronological age of our children as a matter of convenience. Graduation from high school doesn't necessarily mean mental and emotional readiness for college.

• Even when mentally capable, not every child should go to college. A trade or technical school or a first job may be more in line with the needs and aspirations of some. Attempts to persuade teens to go to college when it does not seem right to them may result in false guilt feelings and prolonged unhappiness.

• Self-image is not always an accurate indicator of ability. Fear of failing in college sometimes persists even when there is evidence to the contrary and presumption about academic success is not always borne out.

• Not all college education is the same. A vast difference exists among colleges regarding their moral and academic standards and their educational theory. Do we know what the standards are and do we agree with them? Does a college place a higher priority on "life adjustment skills" or on "intellectual content and discipline"? Is there a balance?

• Questions to ask ourselves: Am I encouraging the development of my teen's talents and interests? Has my teen been examined for aptitudes and interests by the school guidance counselor? Am I encouraging study and reading habits necessary for higher education? If college is not an option, have I helped my teen explore other possibilities for getting desired knowledge and skills, such as correspondence schools, continuing-education seminars, and night or weekend classes? How will my teen's education be funded? Do I know what I need to know to be of help? If not, where can I get the information?

Values to Transfer

As I consider the foundational values about education I would want to pass on to my children, the following come to mind. My list may stimulate you to list your own.

1. Learning can be enjoyable. Letting our minds grapple with difficult concepts and seeming paradoxes and discovering big ideas doesn't need to be drudgery. If we learn how to think and approach the process with a positive attitude, learning really can be fun.

2. Gaining wisdom is a major life goal. It's not just a matter of learning during school. Neither is it just acquiring knowledge for a particular job. Wisdom equips us for the purpose for which we were created, thus we ought to pursue it with gusto and determination in all our reading, observation, and experience of life. In his attempt to transfer this concept to his son, King Solomon wrote:

> My son, if you accept my words . . .
> and if you call out for insight
> and cry aloud for understanding,
> and if you look for it as for silver
> and search for it as for hidden treasure,
> then you will understand the fear of the Lord
> and find the knowledge of God.[2]

3. Wisdom includes a dimension of wonder. The more we know, the more we know that we don't know everything. Far from being a discouraging thought, this is mind-expanding. It helps us to sense our true relationship to the rest of reality—we are almost infinitely small compared to all creation, yet able to commune with the Creator!

4. Education is never complete. It's a life-long process of training the mind, gaining knowledge, seeking the truth. Thus an open mind and teachable spirit are essential. At the same time, we can know some things with certainty without knowing everything. A college freshman doesn't know as much as his professor of philosophy, but he just might have a clearer glimpse of the truth.

5. "Dig deep, irrigate widely." I am indebted for this bit of wisdom to the repeated encouragement of my friend, Dr. Ken Pike, former head of the Linguistics Department at the University of Michigan. The image conveys a value I want to transfer to my children: thinking well may be difficult work, but the deeper we go the broader and more useful the application.

6. Reason and faith are complementary. The scientific process is built on the faith that certain natural laws will continue to hold true, whether they are fully understood or not. Water always boils at 212 degrees at sea level. Gravity always pulls objects heavier than air to the ground. Without faith in natural laws, reason would be useless. The technology that took us to the moon was based on faith in the natural laws of the universe. King Solomon expressed the complementary relationship of faith and reason when he said: "The fear of the Lord (an awe-filled faith) is the beginning of knowledge (a reason-filled wisdom)."[3]

Door-openers to Try

Suppose you hold to similar or perhaps quite different values about education. How do you and I communicate our values in effective ways? Granted, a lot is caught instead of taught, but we can also try "door-openers" that make use of our teens' "moments of readiness" for the transfer of our values.

• Read good books. If something interests you, talk about it. It may spark the reading interest of your teen.

• Share insights. Maybe something you heard or read strikes you as fascinating or as the answer to a puzzling question. Perhaps it opens a new dimension of thought. Tell about it briefly and with enthusiasm.

• Invite questions and comments. Never ridicule a thought from your children. Create an atmosphere in the home where it is safe to express even half-formed ideas, where each thought is treated with respect.

• Talk about news events and invite opinions on topics that may be controversial. Let your children know what you think and why you think that way, but convey genuine openness to their ideas. If you do, conversation will take on the quality of a mutually satisfying discussion and dialogue instead of argument and one-up-manship.

• Admit mistakes of logic or reason. "I guess that doesn't make a whole lot of sense, does it?" "Well, that proves I was wrong." Honesty and humility *increase* credibility.

• Reward discovery. Comment on new insights or logical connections made by your teen.

— That's a neat idea.
— I think that's a profound point.
— I appreciate the way you worked through that math problem.
— The points you make in your term paper are intriguing. For example, I like this one about . . . .
— That sounds interesting. Tell me more.

• Listen actively. Ask questions. Look your teen in the eye and show interest in what your teen is saying. Encourage the development of the thinking process through your comments.

— Have you thought what you would do if . . . ?
— I see. How did you arrive at that conclusion?
— Then what?
— I'm not sure I see the connection.
— Could there be some way to combine your interests in math and psychology?

VOCATION: WHAT WILL I DO WITH MY LIFE?

In one of our "heart-to-heart" talks when Jud was fifteen, he said, "Dad, I don't know what kind of work I should go into. I think about it and try to weigh all the factors, but nothing comes clear. Sometimes I want to know so badly that it hurts, like a pain right here in my chest."

Our teens probably think a lot more about their future than we realize. Much of the thinking . . . and the hurting . . . they will have to experience themselves. Yet parents have asked the big questions about vocation too. Perhaps we are still wondering if we made the right decision, or maybe we're in the process of changing to a new line of work now and we know the pressures. Examining our own experience can prepare us to be of help when our teens ask us, "What will I do with my life? How do I decide? What factors should I consider?"

Points to Ponder about Vocation

• Many people are unhappy in their careers. Surveys have shown that work is most often associated in some people's minds with apathy, boredom, nervousness, shouting matches, and daily humiliations. Management experts estimate that nearly 80 percent of all Americans are dissatisfied with their work and career. Is it because they chose their careers without adequate thought and without a sense of mission?

• Job dissatisfaction can lead to boredom, lack of purpose in life, and even a sense of hopelessness.

• A study by the National Assessment of Educational Progress has concluded that most students in high school today do not have realistic expectations about their careers. Only 35 percent of the seventeen-year-olds said that they had spoken with the school advisor about their career aspirations and plans.

• People skills are essential in most jobs. For professionals and inexperienced workers alike, few problems at work have to do with technical skills, training, knowledge, information, or intelligence. Most problems (85 percent according to one study) are caused by an inability to communicate well with people.

• Informational sources such as *Occupational Outlook Handbook* (U.S. Dept. of Labor), *Encyclopedia of Careers* (Doubleday), and *Dictionary of Occupational Titles* (U.S. Dept. of Labor) are readily available and help to bridge the informational gap our teens have about various careers.

• Extensive surveys conducted by the Institute for Social Research at the University of Michigan suggest that long hours of part-time work by teenagers are linked with weak school performance, low college aspirations, and higher drug use.[4]

Values to Transfer

1. Work can be a positive means of expressing our talents and interests. Contrary to the thinking of some people, work is not a "curse." It's possible to find immense enjoyment and fulfillment in work.

2. The value of work is not determined by the amount of money we receive for it. It's a sad commentary on the priorities of our society that it supports million-dollar contracts for football players but provides bare subsistence for the teachers of our children. A mother's work invested in the lives of her

children is, at the very minimum, as valuable as the work of an athlete or business executive.

3. A sense of mission in our work prevents it from becoming a meaningless routine. The word vocation comes from the Latin word *vocare,* meaning "to call," and refers to the idea that one's work is a "calling" from God. If our teens acquire the understanding that a prospective career is their *calling,* their work will take on a sense of meaning far beyond that produced by mere money or prestige.

4. Any work can be done to the glory of God. The critical point is one's *motive,* whether one works for his own glory or God's glory. Sociological studies suggest that if one's motive in work is ego-centered, the result is likely to be dissatisfaction and lack of fulfillment.[5]

5. Work ought to be characterized by a passion for excellence. If our mission and motive for work are in line, it follows that our method will be one of diligence, a constant and careful attempt to do our best. The Apostle Paul wrote, "Whatever you do, *work heartily,* as serving the Lord" (Colossians 3:23). To work heartily means to put your whole self into your work; aim for the highest standard of which you are capable.

6. Overwork is counterproductive. Perfectionistic and "workaholic" tendencies suggest that work has become the master of life. The result is almost always stress, fatigue, impatience, and neglect of our most important relationships. In addition, the quality of work declines. During the French Revolution, the government decided to do away with "Sabbath Observance" and institute a seven-day work schedule for greater productivity. The experiment failed due to deterioration of the nation's health and decreased motivation of the workers.

Door-openers to Try

• Explore various career interests with your teen. Avoid making judgmental statements like "There's no market for that kind of work" or "I doubt that you could stand the pressure." Qualifying statements and personal reservations may need to be introduced later, but during the early stages of the decision process, explore all possibilities. Keep in mind that our teens need to know that their future work is their decision and responsibility, not ours. They will resist attempts to control, but during their moments of openness will appreciate our attempts to assist.

• Ask questions that help your teen to think through career possibilities.

— What kinds of activities do you feel you are good at? (Mental, manual, interpersonal?)
— What kind of people would you enjoy working with? (Thinkers, practitioners, craftsmen, decision makers, leaders, followers, a combination?)
— What area of the country would you want to settle in? (Near or far away from home, climate, terrain, urban or rural?)
— What kind of hours? (Flexible, strictly 9–5, nights, days?)
— What would your goals be in your work? What would you want to accomplish? What would make you feel good about yourself?

Avoid an attitude or manner of interrogation! These are sensitive questions requiring the right time, place, and attitude. Conveying acceptance, even when you might not agree with your teen's ideas, is critical to effective help.

• Don't kill enthusiasm or overreact to an idea that may seem impossible to you. Trust the process of gathering information, brainstorming about possibilities, examining alternatives, gaining wisdom through experience, and open-ended communication.

• Encourage your teen to take the Strong Vocational Interest Test or some other standard of measurement (perhaps through the school's guidance office) that would serve as an indicator of how your teen's interests compare with those who are successful in their field of endeavor.

• Explore career possibilities. Our family decided to ask friends who work in a variety of careers to come for dinner occasionally. We ask questions like the following:

— What is the nature of your work? What do you actually do from day to day?

— Why did you choose your line of work?
— What were some of the steps that led you to your choice of work?
— If you could make your decision over again, what would you do differently?
— What are some of the problems you encounter in your work? How do you handle them?
— What do you like about your work? What keeps you in it?

Yes, it requires extra effort to plan such encounters, but the resulting discussions are usually fascinating and helpful.

• Talk openly about your own work, your disappointments and sources of satisfaction. If possible, invite your teen to spend a day at work with you and to work alongside you. Treat your teen as you would an esteemed friend or highly valued new employee. Approach the venture with the attitude that your teen is joining the "team" for the day. Think about what your teen might do that would help him or her understand your work.

• Avoid making your teen feel pressured into choosing the same career you did. If that choice were a bad fit, you would be partly responsible for the problems that would likely follow. Besides, such pressure conveys a disregard of the individuality and unique potential of our teens.

• Beware of subtle pressures your teen might feel, such as several generations in your family focusing on a particular line of work. You may have to convince your teen that he or she really is free to choose. If you feel strongly about continuing a family tradition and your teen thinks differently, you might need to struggle long and hard to solve this problem.

• Assist your teen when necessary with the details of job hunting. The "unknown" can seem like an impassable barrier. Help your teen to begin the process in easily manageable chunks (filling out a form, making a telephone call, getting necessary help), *but don't do the work.* One mother made all the calls to an employer and answered all the employer's questions. She taught her daughter nothing, but gave her the impression she wasn't capable of handling the situation by herself. Another mother told her daughter, "I'll stay as close or as far away as you wish. You take the lead. I know you can do it."

• Check the library and bookstore for resources. Consult with the school guidance counselor and others who may be of help. Taking the time to get the right kind of help can prevent days and weeks of aimless exploring.

MONEY: WHAT ARE MY PRIORITIES?

Chuck Colson tells about a man at a car rental counter who loudly insisted that he needed a black Continental because all the other people who were going to his New Year's Eve party that night would be driving black Continentals. On the man's T-shirt was this inscription: "The one who has the most toys when he dies, wins." Did the man really believe that motto? Is it an adequate philosophy for life? Did anyone help him as a young man to sort what his priorities would be?

Points to Ponder about Money

• A growing number of college freshmen are concerned with little other than making a living. According to a twenty-year study by the Cooperative Institutional Research Program (CIRP), accumulating money seems to be especially important. While twenty years ago more than 80 percent of freshmen chose "developing a meaningful philosophy of life" as an essential goal, today only 41 percent consider that a worthy goal. CIRP pollsters Alexander Austin and Kenneth Green observe: "It may be that some students view making a lot of money as a kind of 'philosophy of life' itself."[6]
• If teenagers work a steady job or are freely given money by their parents, they often experience "premature affluence." Thinking they have enough money to buy what they want and adopting the habit of "buy now, pay later," they maintain their spending spree in college and after marriage. The result? Feelings of entrapment, hopelessness, and failure when the extra money sources dry up. In his book, *When All You've Ever Wanted Isn't Enough,* Rabbi Harold Kushner suggests that the theme of Ecclesiastes is supported by contemporary analysis: a

counterproductive attachment to things results in dissatisfaction with life.

• Misunderstandings about priorities can cause people to work a lifetime for money, trying to buy peace of mind and happiness without ever achieving either.

• Media advertising that promises we can have it all is partly responsible for the increased materialism of our society. To avoid being taken prisoner by materialism (thinking we must have the "in thing"), we need to talk openly with our teens about what materialism is and how we try to rise above its grasp.

• Money management is a skill best learned at an early age in the home. We must keep in mind that our teens are more likely to adopt what they see us *do* than what they hear us say.

• Americans earn more per person than any people in the history of the world, yet the overwhelming majority of those who reach 65 have saved little or no money. Only two out of every one hundred are financially independent, twenty-three are forced to continue working just to survive, and seventy-five are dependent on social security, friends, relatives, or charity.[7]

Values to Transfer

1. Seek first the kingdom of God and everything else will fit in its proper perspective.[8]

2. Money is a tool that can be used for good or evil. It is the "love of money" (devotion or commitment to it) that is the root of all evil.[9] If we make money our god, it will plague us like the devil.

3. Gratitude results from realizing that "The earth is the Lord's and everything in it, the world and all who live in it." This means that everything we have the Lord has entrusted to us. We are stewards of what ultimately belongs to him.[10]

4. A grateful heart will give cheerfully to help meet the spiritual and physical needs of others. The standard our family voluntarily and gladly commits to is the "tithe" or one tenth of our income.

5. Stewardship of our resources involves learning the skills of wise planning, budgeting, saving, investing, and giving.

6. If we consciously distinguish between needs and wants, and budget to meet our needs first, we will avoid financial bondage.

7. Contentment is a priceless peace of mind everyone wants but no one can buy. It does not result from self-satisfaction or giving in to things as they are. Rather, it derives from an attitude that enjoys God's providence in the present and uses the resources he has provided to strive for the highest goals in the future.

Door-openers to Try

• Talk with your teen about your financial decisions, including what you have learned from your mistakes as well as your successes.

• Discuss long-range costs. Most teens focus their attention on present needs and wants. It's hard for them to see the long-range consequences of "buy now, pay later."

• Ask your teen to keep a weekly budget sheet for two weeks and to record all income and expenses.

• Mention some biblical principles regarding money and possessions and discuss with your teen what you think the principles mean. Here's a list of seven references and questions for discussion.

Psalm 24:1	— If everything ultimately belongs to God, how does that affect the way we think about things and use money?
Matthew 6:33	— What does it mean for us to seek first God's kingdom? What things do you think will be added? Why is the ordering of our priorities so important?
Philippians 4:12	— How does one learn the secret of contentment? Does "contentment" as it is used here

	mean that one should not strive for more or work for change?
Acts 5:1–11	— Why was the action of Ananias and Sapphira punished so severely? Why does God require us to be honest in the use of our money?
Matthew 25:14–23	— In this story told by Jesus, what do you think is the main point?
Colossians 3:23	— What is the ultimate goal for our work? How does that goal affect our attitude toward money and its use?
Matthew 6:1–4	— What's the point of Jesus' message about giving? How do you think the Heavenly Father will reward us?

MARRIAGE: WHO WILL I MARRY?

It sounds pretty clinical, but psychiatrist Harry Stack Sullivan described love well when he said, "When the satisfaction or security of another person becomes as significant to one as is one's own satisfaction and security, then the state of love exists."[11] Still, for most teens, some questions remain: "If I feel love for more than one person, how will I know which is the right one for me? If I don't have strong feelings for anyone right now, is something wrong with me? What if a friend feels strongly about me, but I don't feel as strongly about that friend? How will I know when I'm ready to marry? Who will I marry?"

Such questions are not easily decided and many smaller decisions must be made before the big one about *who* can be answered. By the time our teenagers are asking these big questions our opportunities for influence may be few, but the little we can do may be just what is needed.

Points to Ponder about Marriage

• "Falling" in and out of love is a normal adolescent activity. Dating provides a valuable experience in interacting with several different personalities and learning about characteristics of a relationship that really matters.

• In psychological terms "like attracts like." One key ingredient in happy marriages is compatibility—similarity in areas such as faith, education, family background, interests, attitudes.

• Considerable evidence suggests that problems in marriage could be detected during the dating period. We can help our teens develop early detection skills by providing them a standard of values with which to discern behavior and character.

• In 1870, one out of every 34 marriages ended in divorce; two generations ago, one in every twelve marriages; in the last generation, one in every three; and at present, almost one out of every two marriages is dissolved (based on statistics from the last ten to fifteen years).

• In a study of 3,000 families, researchers Nick Stinnett and John Defrain found six major characteristics of strong families. They

— are committed to the family
— spend time together
— have good family communication
— express appreciation to each other
— have a spiritual commitment, and
— are able to solve problems in a crisis.[12]

• In a chapter entitled, "You and the Person You May Marry," psychologist Irene Kassorla lists some of the danger signs that signal a bad choice:

— pressure applied by the other
— dissatisfaction with the other's expression of affection
— strong parental disapproval
— constant quarreling and bickering
— recurrent doubts
— desire to make changes in the partner's personality
— disapproval of partner's friends
— a relationship which operates in only one area

— a wish to alter the ambitions, dreams, goals of the partner
— feelings of regret regarding the engagement
— repeated episodes of "breaking the engagement"
— either partner's excessively close attachment to parents
— considering demands of the partner unfair or irrational.[13]

• One study surveyed couples who had been happily married for thirty years or more. The common ingredient? Good communication: the ability to listen well and express thoughts and feelings without fear of reprisal.

• Many teens are confused about the difference between love and infatuation. In response to the plea of one young woman, Ann Landers distinguished the two this way.

> Infatuation leaps into bloom. Love usually takes root and grows one day at a time. Infatuation is accompanied by a sense of uncertainty. You are stimulated and thrilled, but not really happy. You are miserable when he is absent. You can't wait until you see him again.
>
> Love begins with a feeling of security. You are warm with a sense of his nearness, even when he is away. Miles do not separate you. You want him near, but near or far, you know he's yours and you can wait.
>
> Infatuation says, "We must get married right away. I can't risk losing him." Love says, "Don't rush into anything. You are sure of one another. You can plan your future with confidence."[14]

Values to Transfer

1. Abstinence before marriage, faithfulness after marriage. The primary reason for living by these values is not merely that it's smart, safe, or psychologically healthy, however important these reasons are proven to be. The primary reason is that it is God's will.[15] Promiscuity and adultery are sins because they damage God's design for the highest level of personal and interpersonal wholeness.

2. Lifelong commitment. God intends marriage to last as long as both partners shall live.[16] Since emotions are unpredictable, any marriage based on emotion or erotic feeling alone is likely to fail. "As long as we both shall love" never has the strength or staying power as the commitment "as long as we both shall live."

3. Marital oneness. A "pair bonding" takes place when a man and a woman choose to leave their parents and create a new identity together, a new union. Note that in Genesis 2:24, the "cleaving" to one's spouse requires "leaving" one's parents. As parents, we need to communicate to our children that we view their marriage as a major transition, a shift from parental allegiance to a new allegiance to their spouse, and that we will not hold them back from their leaving by our clinging.

4. Compatibility. Marital intimacy results from hard work. It's a work of the heart, mind, soul, and will. Even when several indicators of compatibility converge and point in the same direction, it's still not easy. Indicators that are most promising include the following:

— A shared faith which the couple practices together
— A developing love for the other which each communicates daily in ways that each partner understands and appreciates
— A commitment to each other for life
— Ease in talking honestly about thoughts and feelings
— Mutual respect and admiration for each other's character
— A caring relationship willing to compromise self-interest to promote the other's happiness
— Compatibility in goals and plans for family, vocation, lifestyle, and financial priorities
— Ability to resolve conflicts
— A willingness and readiness to forgive
— A shared sense of humor.

5. Trust. Adequate time is required for couples to evaluate their readiness for the complexity and demands of marriage. They need time to build a strong foundation of deep understanding, trust, and mutual goals.

6. Communication. A commitment to practicing good communication prevents the normal development of bad communication habits. It bridges differences and promotes the experience of oneness. With such a commitment, the ease and intrigue of talking with each other that most couples experience *before* marriage will continue *after* marriage. The couple's communication will be characterized by openness, sensitivity, mutual fulfillment, and the sheer joy of knowing . . . and being known by . . . a "significant other."

Door-openers to Try

• When your teen seems interested, share your own search for "the right one" to marry. Include the humor, the mistakes, the feelings, hopes, and dreams, but don't get carried away and talk forever. Sparkle. Let your teen ask for more.

• Encourage your teen to consider what characteristics in a potential mate are important. In *Skills for Living,* the Quest National Center lists the following fourteen characteristics of a potential marriage partner.[17] Ask your teen how he or she would rank each item.

_____ attractiveness
_____ similar religious beliefs and practices
_____ traditional height patterns (the woman the same size or shorter than the man, but not taller)
_____ similar hobbies and recreational activities
_____ intellectual compatibility
_____ similar values regarding food and clothing styles
_____ similar economic backgrounds
_____ similar political beliefs
_____ the support and acceptance of both families
_____ same race and ethnic backgrounds
_____ you like his/her friends and they like you
_____ similar views about having and raising children
_____ similar work interests
_____ ability to communicate and solve problems

Keep in mind that this is just an exercise and the ranking is likely to change. Be careful not to judge their answers and cut off communication. Our aim needs to be to listen intelligently and lead them in their self-discovery of what is noble, true, excellent, and worthy of praise.

• Provide books which help teens to ask themselves good questions. Sensitive suggestions and directing them to selected resources can calm anxieties about many unknowns, such as the fear of not finding the right mate.

• When your teen is in a talkative mood about marriage, ask questions or make statements in a nonthreatening way that keep your teen talking, discovering, learning. You can say:

— This relationship seems really important to you.
— I sense that you are troubled by the way Ken talks to you.
— I've never seen you so excited about anyone as you are about Kimberly. She seems very special.
— You've talked about a number of characteristics you are looking for in a marriage partner. Which do you think are most important to a healthy marriage?

• Talk about the barriers to marital oneness that you have experienced and how you have tried to overcome these barriers. Some teens have unrealistic expectations about marriage. They need to know that there are likely to be difficulties and that it takes a strong commitment to work through them.

• Talk about your values. After thinking through what you believe is important for a happy marriage, aim for dialogue by encouraging your teen's questions and listening intently.

• Discuss key Scripture passages related to marriage:

—Genesis 2:18–25	Companionship, unity, total acceptance
—Proverbs 31:10–31	Noble characteristics in a wife (Reflect on similar characteristics in a husband.)
—1 Corinthians 13	The famous love chapter
—Ephesians 5:21–32	Mutual submission, love, honor
—1 Peter 3:1–7	Submission, consideration, respect

• When it seems appropriate, pray about your children's future marriage within their hearing. Some teens never hear their parents pray for them and they miss a great source of strength and guidance. Pray for your teen and for the person your teenager will one day marry.

> Heavenly Father, I ask your blessing not only upon my son/daughter, but also upon the one whom he/she will someday marry. Even now keep them in the center of your will. When they marry, grant them the grace of a life-long commitment to each other. May their love be strengthened with a growing respect. May they be ever ready to forgive and bring out the best in each other. May they keep the channels of communication open in difficult times as well as times of ease. O God, may their faith in you enable them to rise above their difficulties and experience the joy and sacredness of life together.
> Amen.

FAITH: WHAT WILL I BELIEVE?

In *The Closing of the American Mind,* Allan Bloom notes that at one time the family was the true center of religious training.

> My grandparents were ignorant people by our standards. But their home was spiritually rich because all things done in it found their origin in the Bible's commandments. Their simple faith and practices linked them to the great thinkers who dealt with the same material.[18]

According to Bloom, if students today come to the university with no sense of "the great revelations, epics and philosophies," part of the reason is that "the dreariness of the family's spiritual landscape passes belief."[19]

Why be moral? Why should I act any differently than my classmates? Why should I not act the way I feel at the moment? Although we can give several answers when teens ask these questions, the answer that emerges powerfully from all the rest is the motivation of faith in a personal God who has revealed how he wants us to live.

Points to Ponder about Faith

• According to one study, 43 percent of the parents and youth never discuss God, the Bible, or spiritual things as a family. Thirty-two percent do so twice a month, and 13 percent once a week. That leaves only 12 percent who regularly discuss matters of faith at home.[20]

• Moral behavior, service activities, and fewer self-destructive practices are found among young people who say their faith is "central and important."[21]

• On the basis of their study, Merton and Irene Strommen report that "adolescents with a liberating faith—that is, who understand the gospel as a gift of salvation through Christ—not only show wholesome behavior, but also are less racially prejudiced and less likely to be involved in such antisocial activities as fighting, vandalism, shoplifting, cheating at school, or lying to parents."[22]

• Due to increasing doubt during the adolescent years, teenagers need an opportunity to express doubts and ask questions in a context that encourages rather than stifles their spiritual journey. Said one young adult about her youth group and leader: "I was confused in my beliefs as a teenager and said some rather blasphemous things, but the group cared enough to hear me out, and because of its acceptance and understanding, I am today a believer in Christ and his Word."[23]

• Religious interest may decline during early adolescence, reaching its lowest point among ninth-grade boys. Since adolescence is a time of discovery, we can also anticipate that our teens will show new interest in attempting to understand the mystery of a relationship with the Creator of the universe. This interest can be enhanced by parental leadership in discussing faith in the family.

• In an article on building faith in our children, Kenneth S. Kantzer wisely said: "Our task is not to make our children into our own image, but to make them into the image of Christ. That means our goal is not to instruct them precisely in what we know to be right, but to enable them to become self-instructing persons who make their own decisions in the light of the Word of God."[24]

• Two factors are linked with a liberating, challenging, outgoing faith, say Merton and Irene Strommen. "One is a parental pattern that includes trust, spending time together as a family, and expressing love. The other is a democratic-authoritative style of control."[25]

• Teenagers want to know the spiritual pilgrimage of their parents. They will be drawn to faith if it is an everyday part of life, not only a Sunday routine.

• Parents' faith significantly influences the faith of their children. If the parent's faith is positive (characterized by genuine devotion, honesty, repentance, and grateful obedience), the teenager's faith is likely to reflect the same character. Some teens will rebel regardless of the quality of faith in their parents, but I believe that the rebellion creates a cognitive dissonance in the mind and heart of the teen who is brought up in a home where faith in Christ is strong and honestly practiced. That dissonance causes an uneasiness that may eventually drive the child back to the faith of his/her father and mother.[26]

Values to Transfer

1. Grace. Eternal life is a free gift. We can't earn it or deserve it. "By grace you have been saved, through faith—and this not from yourselves, it is the gift of God—not by works" (Ephesians 2:8).

2. Man. Because of sin, we cannot earn eternal life. "There is no one who is righteous, not even one. All have sinned and fall short of the glory of God" (Romans 3:10, 23).

3. God. The nature of God includes both his love and his holiness. Because of his holiness, God must punish sin. Because of his love, God has provided a way to escape the penalty of sin. "The wages of sin is death, but the gift of God is eternal life in Christ Jesus our Lord" (Romans 6:23).

4. Christ. More than a man, Christ is the infinite God-man, fully man and fully divine. "In the beginning was the Word (Christ), and the Word was with God, and the Word was God . . . . The Word became flesh and lived for a while among us. We have seen his glory, the glory of the one and only Son, who came from the Father, full of grace and truth" (John 1:1, 14). By his death on the cross, Christ paid the penalty for our sin and purchased a place for us in heaven, which he offers to us as a free gift. "God demonstrates his own love for us in this: While we were still sinners, Christ died for us. Since we

have now been justified by his blood, how much more shall we be saved from God's wrath through him" (Romans 5:8–9).

5. Faith. We receive the gift of eternal life by faith. Faith is a turning from sin and trusting in Jesus Christ alone for salvation. "For God so loved the world that he gave his one and only Son, that whoever believes in him shall not perish but have eternal life" (John 3:16).[27]

Door-openers to Try

• Create an atmosphere of openness about your faith. Let your children know that your faith in God is real to you by expressing your own questions and insights, your struggles and your gratitude.

• Allow the *adventure* of faith to shine through. When faith in God is at the center of our lives, it affects every dimension of need. I will never forget the way my parents demonstrated this. When I was six I desperately wanted a bike, but since we had a large family and my father was a preacher, we did not have enough money to buy one. In her book, *Consecrated Hands,* my mother tells the story:

> One morning at the breakfast table after we had just finished our family prayers, and each of the children had prayed that in some way Paul would be able to have a bike, there was a knock at the door. It was our next door neighbor, who said, "Bill wants to sell his bike, but before he puts an ad in the paper he wondered if Paul might be interested in having it. He will charge Paul only $5.00." I wish you could have seen the eyes of our children. Why, God had answered their prayers that very morning![28]

God doesn't always answer prayer like that. Good thing. The next morning I started praying for a horse. However, the point my parents impressed upon me from childhood was that we can talk to God about anything, that he cares about children as well as adults. It was natural then as a teenager to sense that in the midst of ordinary events was the dimension of an extraordinary God who cared even about me.

• Pray for direction in decision-making. When my family and I considered a move to Memphis, Tennessee, Jud and Jessica pointed out that they would have to leave lifetime friends. Eight-year-old Jessica said, "Dad, we have no relatives in

Memphis and if we move there I will never have any friends again." For several days we talked and prayed about it as a family. Then at the dinner table one night I said that it was time to make a decision. I asked each member of the family the same question, beginning with Jessica. "On the basis of what you know about this decision, Jessica, do you think that it is God's will that we go to Memphis?" Through her tears, she said "Yes!" The family's sense of God's will was unanimous. When we arrived in Memphis, we found that there were five friends Jessica's age on our street. Having prayed for direction, she knew whom to thank.

• Read the Bible together as a family. My parents read Bible stories with enthusiasm and expression, as if they were the greatest stories ever told. Often we listened with rapt attention to the high drama of David and Goliath, Samson and the Philistines, Daniel in the lions' den, the conversion of the Apostle Paul, the crucifixion and resurrection of Jesus Christ. As we grew older, we sensed the depth of feeling in the Psalms, the search for an adequate philosophy of life described by Solomon, the amazing authority of Jesus Christ demonstrated in the Gospels, the divine power evident in miracles. Gradually we began to realize that all redemptive history really is *His-story*, and for some reason beyond comprehension, solely by grace, through faith, he wants to include us in the eternal blessing.

ACTION STEPS FOR POSITIVE COMMUNICATION

1. Select one of the five decision areas (Education, Vocation, Money, Marriage, or Faith) that you feel is most important to your teen at this time. Write down a few "door-openers" that you feel might work and begin talking to your teen about this matter. It is important to be relaxed and sensitive to the interest level of your teen.

2. Determine in which of the five decision areas you need to reassess your own values. Set a goal related to your sense of need. My goal in the area of _____ is to

_____.

3. If your teen needs additional help or information in making a major decision, decide what you can do to help your teen get the needed information. My plan is to _____

_____.

I hate to say it, but my parents don't talk much to me or it's the other way around. We're just like animals not knowing how to speak or show emotion. I don't blame my parents or myself, because that's the way we were raised. But in the future, I hope our communication will be better.

—Jane (17)

Five Messages Teens Want to Hear (Jud's Chapter)

When I asked over 800 teenagers what "messages" they really wanted to hear from their parents, some of the responses did not surprise me at all.

— Go have fun!
— We will buy you a car when you're sixteen—and pay for the insurance.
— You don't have to take out the garbage anymore.
— Be in whenever you feel like it.
— Here's that five hundred dollars you wanted.
— Since you're too tired to get up, I'll have your brother do your chores.
— I love it when your room is messy!

Those were the fun messages. The messages teenagers said they actually receive from their parents reflect the daily conflicts that can make home life such a hassle. Here are some classic examples:

— You had better get good grades or you will mess up your entire life!
— You're grounded for a month! . . . Make that two months!
— Turn off the TV, go to your room, and study.
— I don't care if everyone else does it. If everyone else jumped off the Empire State Building, would you?
— When I was your age . . . .
— Where are you going? With whom? Who's driving? When will you be home? Wear your seatbelt. Be careful!
— Get off the phone!
— Because I said so and that's final.

As the authority figure, the parent has every "right" to say such things, but do these messages produce a positive or negative response from teens? In this chapter I describe the messages that teens feel will increase communication and can strengthen your relationship with them.

In my survey I asked teenagers what they most wanted to hear from their parents. From their responses, five messages stand out. All the quotes used in this chapter are typical and represent a large number of similar responses.

1. "I'M PROUD OF YOU"

Do you remember how good it felt when your parents said, "I'm proud of you"? Maybe your parents rarely told you how proud they were and you remember how bad that felt. Maybe your parents complimented you on your appearance or accomplishments, but never actually said the words, "I'm proud of you."

I wish my parents would just tell me they're proud of me instead of always being so hard on me. It seems like I never do anything right and when I do, they tell me I could have done better.

—Charla (16)

I want to hear them say that I am a great daughter, that I'm just what they wanted, and that they are proud of me.

—Kelly (13)

I wish that when I bring home good grades, ribbons, or awards, they would tell me that they are proud of me.

—Brian (17)

For once, I wish my mother would be proud of me for the grades I make. For example, if I try my hardest and make a B, she still wants me to make an A.

—Sherrin (16)

All these teenagers are looking to fulfill one basic need: approval. Ever since we can remember we have sought the praise of our parents and the people whom we respect. After a preschooler draws a picture, he runs to Mommy for approval. If an elementary school student makes an A on a test, he is sure to tell Mom and Dad about it because their approval is certain. A junior high school student may get an unorthodox haircut because it meets with his peers' approval. A high school student seeks approval from members of the opposite sex. But during the teenage years, parental approval is perhaps most important to a teenager because it is the key to forming an identity and building positive self-esteem.

A parent's pride should be related to a teenager's effort and ability as an individual, not compared with anyone else. If a teen tries out for football and attends every practice, it should not matter to the parent if he spends every game on the bench. If a teen goes out for cross-country and runs each race as fast as he can, it should not matter whether he comes in first or last. If a daughter performs in a play, the size of her part should not make any difference. You see, pride in one's child is not related to points scored, yards run, winning or losing. "I'm proud of you," can be said any time teenagers—

- choose to put in an extra effort to achieve a personal goal
- choose to overcome peer pressure and make their own decisions

- determine to learn from mistakes and try again
- use their natural abilities to the fullest.

Dr. Victor B. Cline in his book *How to Make Your Child a Winner* says that kids are lazy because their parents permit it.[1] I believe this is true. Motivating one's child is an important job of parents. A parent can influence a younger child to practice piano for fifteen minutes every day. When the child plays his first song, the parent will be able to be proud of that child, even though the parent had to make the child persevere long enough to learn the song. The child's early success and the approval of parents will begin to build an inner desire that eventually will cause the child to become self-motivated. This strategy can be applied to teenagers. Parents who retain their authority have the power to influence their teens' actions. Parents must try to develop positive qualities in their teens through the careful use of parental authority, discipline, and positive motivation. Then they can say to their teen, as if he or she alone had done all the work, "I'm proud of you."

If teens think that they have to make all A's to be accepted by their parents, they may feel that their parents are only concerned about success and not about them as persons. As a result they may not try to do their best. This may be why some teens with superior ability do just enough to get by. Although parents cannot be proud of their teens' behavior when they fail to perform to their potential, they should never, never, withhold love. The feeling of being loved is generally needed more during times of failure than times of success.

When teens make wrong decisions or fail to do their best, it is difficult to be proud of their actions. Although an "I'm proud of you" message may be inappropriate in such instances, parents can still affirm their teenagers as persons. Try to make the distinction between the actions and the person. You can still be proud of the person even when his actions do not express his best self.

Teens want a general bank of approval based on who they are as persons, not on daily performances. Then when they fail, they can draw from that bank for self-esteem. When a teen fails, never say, "I am not proud of you" or "You will never amount to anything." A simple slip of the tongue like that can be devastating to your teen. In effect it says, "I'm disappointed in you as a person." This message really hurts because a teen may not merely think that he has failed in some action, but that he has failed as a person. Such thoughts crush self-esteem and carry a sense of permanence that can snuff out the motivation needed to strive for excellence. Parents need to accept teens when they fail so that they can rebuild their confidence and try again. They must make it plain by what they say that it is only their teens' *actions* that disappoint them.

An "I'm proud of you" message encourages teenagers to set higher goals and fuels their desire to reach those aims. It raises self-esteem and gives confidence. Don't miss a single opportunity to say, "I'm proud of you."

2. "YOU CAN ALWAYS COME TO ME WITH ANYTHING AND I WILL BE THERE TO LISTEN"

I think we would all agree that good listening is the first step to good communication. Teenagers consider this a great message because it assures them that the first and hardest step will be taken. A parent's failure to listen is a major reason teens keep things to themselves. Can you afford to miss what you may be missing?

> If I knew my parents would really listen to me, I would tell them how much I love them and appreciate them. I would tell them that I know they work hard to get me some of the things I want. I would also tell them that when I graduate and move out, I will never forget what they have done for me.
> —Brian (15)
>
> If my parents would really listen to me, I would tell them all my problems and tell them how I feel. I would also tell them that I rely on them to listen to my problems and to help me solve them.
> —Brandon (15)
>
> If my father would listen with an open heart and not judge my feelings by how young I am, then I would love dearly to tell him how much I love Allen (my boyfriend), how special he is to me, how he makes me so happy. I wish he could understand and feel the joy I have when I'm with Allen.
> —Susanne (15)

If my parents would really listen to me, I would tell them that I am sorry for any pain I have caused them and that I love them. I would tell them that I would do anything in the world for them.

—Melinda (16)

In the chapter, "Getting through to Teens," you read about "Earning the Right to Be Heard." I call the following basic rules of listening "Earning the Right to Be Told." The responses from my survey suggest that these rules are essential to getting your teens to talk to you. They underscore the kind of listening that teenagers expect from their parents.

1. *Give undivided attention.* This means to stop cooking, stop reading the newspaper, stop watching TV or thinking about other things and concentrate on what your teen says.

2. *Do not talk when you are trying to listen.* A good listener is not always talking. Empathy is sometimes best communicated by intentional silence and focused attention.

3. *Do not ridicule.* Teenagers have many impractical dreams or ideas, but some of them are fresh and challenging. You will not get a chance to hear them if you are notorious for criticism.

4. *Listen with a willingness to understand.* Simply make complete understanding of your teen a goal and strive to reach that goal.

When you listen in this way, you communicate the following messages without opening your mouth:

"You are important to me."
"I care about the things you are interested in."
"I enjoy listening to your thoughts, ideas, and opinions."
"I love you."

Listening is rewarding because your teen will easily sense these messages when the listening is genuine. Good listening increases your teen's willingness to talk, strengthens the relationship between you, builds mutual trust and respect, and generates love. Saying, "You can come to me with anything . . ." not only sets the foundation for a strong relationship but keeps it going. Further, misunderstandings, wrong assumptions, and frustrations are greatly decreased, if not eliminated.

If active listening on your part is increased, the quality of listening on your teen's part will also increase. Imagine the positive impact it would have on the quality of conversation in your home.

It is also important to point out the dangerous effects of not listening. When parents do not listen, or give the impression that they are not listening, teens may infer the following negative messages from their parents:

"You are not that important to me."
"I couldn't care less about what you are interested in."
"I'd rather be somewhere else."
"I don't really love you enough to listen to you."

Of course, most parents do not mean to imply such messages, but they are easy to convey. Be aware that such inattentive listening immediately destroys conversation and tends to keep future conversations from happening.

Listening is so important to your teen that it is worth making a conscious effort to give your full attention when your teen is talking. If your schedule or energy level make listening difficult, explain that to your teen and ask if the subject can wait until a later designated time. Be sensitive to the fact that the topic might need immediate attention. Because your teen might have a hard time expressing the importance of a topic in words, consider facial expressions, actions, tone of voice, and emotional intensity. Your teen may need to talk about something but not realize it. If he has a hard time finding an audience it would be easy to just say, "Forget it." Then strong feelings are dangerously suppressed. Realize that in such a situation if you do not put your teen first, you may have your priorities mixed up. If you put your teen first, you will be rewarded for making the extra effort because your teen will sense the sacrifices you have made for him and those positive listening messages will come through all the stronger.

Many times teenagers will simply not talk with their parents about certain topics regardless of a parent's communication skill or willingness to listen. In the survey I asked teens: "What keeps you from discussing your deep feelings or personal problems with your parents?" Most answered that they would like to but . . .

I really don't want to cry in front of my mother. I'm afraid to make her feel like she has failed in teaching me things and raising me up.

—Jeffrey (17)

I guess I'm afraid that they won't be proud of me anymore. I don't want to disappoint them after all the wonderful things they have done for me.

—Susan (17)

I realize they say they are always there if I need to talk to them, but would they really understand the way I feel?"

—Cindy (16)

When teens do not talk freely about their problems, parents can still indirectly help them by referring them to a third party. A parent may suggest a youth pastor, a relative, or a close friend of the family. Before there is a problem, say to your teen, "I want you to know that I am always here to listen to you, but if you ever have something that you feel that you can't talk to me about for some reason, please talk to _____ about it. He has agreed to keep everything you say confidential, even from me. He will try to help you the best he can if you should ever need it. OK?"

The teenager may only shrug his shoulders in response, but when he needs to he will remember what you said.

3. "I UNDERSTAND YOU" OR "I WANT TO UNDERSTAND"

I don't think she would understand my personal problems because she is so much older than I and probably has forgotten what it was like when she was a teen.

—Patty (16)

When teens say to their parents, "You don't understand!" they may mean one of two things. They may mean, "I am angry because you do not agree with me" or "You don't know how I am feeling." The first step for parents is to discern what their teens mean when they say, "You don't understand!"

When teens define understanding as agreeing, there will be a "misunderstanding" every time there is a disagreement. "You don't understand" can be used as a weapon against parents and an excuse for not talking. I can picture a well-meaning parent who is trying to be loving and firm but also fair, and the teen runs out of the room yelling, "You just don't understand!" How frustrating for the parent.

But also imagine a teenager sitting alone in his room plagued by a problem of epic proportions. It is the second week in a row that the girl of his dreams is going out with someone else. He is afraid that his parents would not sense the same gravity of the situation and not take him seriously. He is afraid his parents will not understand.

> I guess I think my parents won't understand or that maybe they will laugh at me and tell me how small my problems are compared to theirs.
>
> —Charla (16)

Every teenager is different but the emotions he or she feels are generally the same. To understand your teenager, try to identify the emotions and relate them to the situation and personality of your teen. Try to remember when your topics of discussion consisted of who's going out with whom, unfair teachers, impossible tests, and weekend plans. This will help you relate, but don't expect a 100 percent success rate. Sometimes teenagers don't understand themselves either. Times have changed and teens face many new challenges. Teenagers cannot expect their parents to understand all their feelings but if they know you try, it will be a big help.

Here are three goals to aim for when trying to reach an understanding with your teen:

1. Let the teenager know that you understand him or her even when there is a differing of views.

2. Discover all the motives and desires behind a certain problem or request before forming an opinion.

3. Try to reverse the accusation of not "understanding" into an awareness of your empathy by expressing that your desire to understand is based on the love and concern you have for your teen.

Unfortunately, conveying understanding is complicated. Cheap understanding can backfire. If you say to your teen, "Honey, I know exactly how you feel," chances are you will get an "Oh no you don't!" response. If you are charged with not understanding, ask your teen to help you understand. If it is a matter of disagreement, state what your teen has said to his satisfaction and then restate your views. If it is a matter of not identifying with how your teen feels, your teen will at least know that you are trying your best to understand.

4. "I TRUST YOU"

> The most damaging thing my parents ever said to me was when they told me they could never trust me again.
> —Pam (18)
> I wish my mom would put some trust in me and maybe tell me that she trusts me, has faith in me, and thinks that sometimes I act responsible instead of telling me I'm always irresponsible and immature.
> —Kris (17)

If understanding is complicated, trust is risky. In any situation there are two ways trust can be used. It can veil unacceptable behavior from an unsuspecting parent, or trust can strengthen a relationship by increasing a mutual level of confidence and openness. These are two typical responses to the survey question, "Do you take advantage of your parents' trust?"

> Yes. I will say to my parents, "Will you please trust me on this," and then I will go out and do the thing I told them to trust me on.
> —Anonymous
> No. I have my own morals and standards and I tell my parents what I do, even when I think they might disagree. We talk about it and usually work things out. I need my parents' trust in order to believe in myself.
> —Susan (17)

Trust develops gradually on the basis of acquired knowledge and past experiences. You simply would not trust your thirteen-year-old with your new car because, aside from his driving being illegal, your teen has no knowledge or personal experience that would allow you to trust his judgment.

Temptations can overwhelm one's better judgment. Parents have surely experienced this firsthand, and this fact prevents parents from giving unlimited trust to their children. In fact, parents would not be doing their jobs if they allowed their child to enter situations where the degree of temptation is higher than that child's level of maturity.

Let's look at an example where there is a disagreement between the parent and the teen about curfew. The teen says, "Don't you trust me?" The parent is stuck. He doesn't want to say that he does not trust his teen and yet that seems to be the case. A great response would sound something like this: "Son, I do trust your intentions but staying out past twelve o'clock increases the temptations you face. I would not be doing my job as a parent if I allowed you to be in a situation where the temptations are greater than you can handle and so I must set a few limits."

A balance must be achieved. Some degree of trust must be given in order for that trust to be proven. Always be sure to give that second chance (not necessarily without consequences) when your teen has failed and is truly sorry.

When parents say, "I trust you," it is an especially important message for the teenager. It assures teens that they are trustworthy. They remember that message and think, "My parents trust me." It will make them want to live up to your trust. It also boosts their self-esteem and gives them the feeling that they are growing up.

5. "I LOVE YOU"

Dr. William Glasser in his book *Reality Therapy* breaks down the causes of mental illness into the frustration of the two basic needs: to love, and to be loved.[2] In spite of the great importance of these needs, parents sometimes miss opportunities to express love as well as receive it because the communication of love is not a conscious goal. On the basis of my survey, "I love you" was the most requested message of all.

I wish my parents would say to me every day, not just every other day, that they love me and that they are proud of me.
—Ken (13)

I wish my dad would say, "I love you," more. I think he thinks I'd be embarrassed if my friends heard him, but I definitely would not.

—Susan (17)

I want to hear that they will always love me no matter how I do in life, whether I succeed or fail.

—Brian (15)

I would like to hear that my dad loves me. He never tells me that. It hurts when your own parents don't tell you that they love you. When I have children, I will tell them I love them even when I punish them or even when they make mistakes. I would tell them that I also make mistakes and that I am not perfect.

—David (14)

Love is the essential ingredient in healthy family relationships. The other four messages can never replace the need for love. Teenagers need to feel love communicated and demonstrated. How can teens be certain that they are loved if they are never told? How can teens feel certain that they are loved if their parents never spend time with them?

Some parents may think that they show love through material gifts. They may find a sense of satisfaction in giving these gifts, but then become hurt when their teens don't show gratitude or seem satisfied. The problem might be that what seems like a clear expression of love to the parent may be viewed by the teen as a substitute for love. Instead of a new fishing pole, a son may prefer that his dad take the time to go fishing with him. Instead of having her mother rush off to buy the latest fashion for her, a daughter may prefer that her mother relax, sit down at the kitchen table, and just talk. The way to spell demonstrated love with your teenagers is T-I-M-E.

Of course, love includes more than just spending time with your teen. You might not find a great deal of love demonstrated among family members on a family vacation after they have spent six hours in a car together. Love also includes certain attitudes and behaviors. The most comprehensive definition of love can be found in 1 Corinthians 13. "Love is patient, love is kind. . . . It is not rude, it is not self-seeking, it is not easily angered, it keeps no record of wrongs. . . . It always protects, always trusts, always hopes, always perseveres."[3]

Patience is letting your teen finish saying what is on his mind. It is not getting angry at unintended mistakes. It includes allowing your teen the time needed to grow up.

Kindness is talking and listening to your teen the way you would to your best friend. It is never making fun of your teen when he or she is serious.

Not being rude is providing common courtesy. It's refusing to yell, call your teen names, or engage in put-downs.

Not easily angered is being firm without being insulting. It's caring enough to exercise self-control. It's remembering one's own mistakes.

Keeping no record of wrongs means not bombarding your teen with the guilt of past mistakes. It means forgiving and forgetting.

Persevering is hanging on when your teen is obnoxious, dogmatic, smart-mouthed, and so on.

* * * * *

Keeping in mind what your teens most want to hear will guarantee you better communication. Express your pride, verbalize your willingness to listen with an open mind, state your desire to understand, assure them of your trust, and always remind them of your unconditional love.

Life is an adventure in forgiveness.[1]

—Norman Cousins, *Human Options*

Postscript: A Word of Encouragement

Early in the writing of this book I felt discouraged by the magnitude of the challenge and the feeling that I had not made any headway. Since this was a joint project with my son, I decided to discuss the matter with him. According to my journal entry, the conversation went like this:

Me: Jud, the writing is not going well. Do you think I should give it up?

Jud: Well, Dad . . . I know you may be feeling bad that you haven't made more progress. It's like your mind is in a traffic jam. There are too many things you have to do right now. When the traffic clears, you'll be able to write again.

Me: Hmmm . . . that's a nice thought.

Jud: Besides, did you ever feel this way when you were writing your first book?

Me: Yes, several times.

Jud: OK, then you know you can get over this obstacle too!

I felt encouraged.

Another time I was angry and expressed it to the family. I don't remember what the problem was, but I have in front of me a letter written that evening by my daughter, who is fast approaching the teenage years:

Dear Dad,

Remember the "Super Dad" poem I wrote for you? You are a super dad. And nobody likes it when you are mad, not even you. *I LOVE YOU!* I hope you feel better soon.

Love,

Jessica

P.S. I have a hug for you when you want one.

I felt forgiven.

It is my hope that this book encourages you as much as these responses from my children encourage me . . . for no one is bruise proof, especially not parents. It may be that you have been hurt by what your children have said and done. Shakespeare said, "How sharper than a serpent's tooth it is to have a thankless child."[2] When teenagers seem thankless, when they take their adolescent turmoil out on us, when they become skillful at making us feel we have failed, when they hurt themselves through inappropriate or wrong behavior, we hurt. But regardless of how badly we might feel at times, *pessimism is not really an option.* The prodigal may yet come home. The Saul may one day be converted to a Paul. The Mary Magdalene may still choose the most excellent way. We don't know enough to be pessimistic.

Let us think about what we do know. We know that our children are a gift of God.[3] We know that they will grow up . . . yes, they will grow up. And we know that adolescence presents the greatest challenge and strain on relationships—for them and for us. Parenting adolescents is like climbing the rough side of a mountain. Sometimes we take one step forward and slip two steps back. But with perseverance, one day we will stand with our teens on the mountain top and think . . . *no problem!*

To reach the top, we have examined together twelve goals that get us back on track when we have lost our way and keep us going when the going gets tough. I encourage you now to repeat these goals as an affirmation of the direction that you want to go. You may not have achieved these goals yet, but saying them in the present tense testifies to your determination to reach your destination.

1. I accept the challenge of communicating with my teen.
2. I keep in mind the developmental stresses of adolescence.
3. I do what I need to do to get through to my teen.
4. I listen in ways that motivate my teen to talk to me.
5. I know how communication works and what to do when it doesn't.
6. I respond CALMLY to strong emotions.
7. I exercise parental authority effectively because I have learned the art of knowing when and how to say No . . . and Yes.
8. I acknowledge the importance of temperament in communicating with my teen.
9. I confront the major problems of teenagers effectively.
10. I follow a model for the resolution of conflicts.
11. I talk to my teen about life's major decisions.
12. I communicate five messages my teen wants to hear.

We must believe we can succeed in reaching these goals because fear of failing produces half-hearted attempts. Perhaps the greatest danger we face is the unconscious assumption that our communication patterns as well as those of our teens will remain the same, that the future holds no promise. We must get rid of such assumptions for they can hold us back and prevent us from pursuing opportunities for positive direction.

Imagine that you have at your side a wonderful counselor—one who will listen to every difficulty, give you inner strength to carry your burden, gently but firmly direct you in the way that leads to everlasting wholeness, and enable you to experience the thrilling truth that "life is an adventure in forgiveness." I have found such a counselor in Jesus Christ, and have been surprised by the adventure.

For me and my family, part of the adventure—the risk and the joy—is saying, "I'm sorry" and "I forgive you." We have found that our family cannot function at an optimum level without forgiveness from God and the daily practice of forgiveness in the home.

Forgiveness is the ultimate means of encouragement. If we are sorry for the mistakes we have made in our relationships with our children, we can ask God for forgiveness, receive it, and experience vital change through faith in Christ. We may have to bear the consequences of past actions, but the good news is that the past need not keep us from becoming like the Father, seeking, waiting, drawing his prodigal children home.

With Gratitude

Jud and I want to acknowledge our special indebtedness to the following:

—the 800-plus teenagers who responded to our survey from Ridgeway and Sheffield High Schools in Memphis, Tennessee; Westminster Academy in Fort Lauderdale, Florida; and Fieldston High School in Germantown, New York;

—George Froehlich, Eva Miller, Sue Pettinga, and Bee Shira who assisted in the editing of the manuscript;

—James and Kate Boone, Paul and Dixie Husband, Bryan and Ginny Nearn, Jim and Ruth Remeur, and Tom and Brokke Shipmon—parents of teens and pre-teens—who served as a primary resource group and contributed many helpful suggestions for the improvement of the manuscript;

—Clinical psychologists Chuck Hannaford, Doug Hart, Rich Luscomb, and Paul Neal for their valuable input and critical review of the manuscript;

—my parents and each of my five sisters, Ethelanne, Marcia, Karen, Faith, and Mary, who helped me appreciate the benefits of good communication and encouraged me in the writing of this book;

—Janiece and Jessica, who daily gave Jud and me enough love and support to get us over writer's block and reach our goal.

Paul and Judson Swets
1132 Longreen Drive
Memphis, TN 38119

Notes

Preface: A Personal Invitation to Parents
1. *USA Today,* 4/13/87, 1.

Chapter 1
1. Bill Cosby, *Fatherhood* (Garden City: Doubleday, 1986), 81.
2. Harry Emerson Fosdick, quoted in Dorothy Sarnoff, *Make the Most of Your Best* (New York: Doubleday & Co., Inc., 1981), 1.
3. Dorothy Sarnoff, 4.

Chapter 2
1. David Elkind, *All Grown Up & No Place to Go* (Reading, MA: Addison-Wesley Publishing Co., 1984), 99.
2. Erik H. Erikson, ed., *The Challenge of Youth* (New York: Doubleday & Co., Inc., 1965), 10.
3. David Elkind, 6–8.
4. Bruce Narramore, *Adolescence Is Not an Illness* (Old Tappan, New Jersey: Fleming H. Revell Co., 1980), 61.
5. Wizard of Id Cartoon, News America Syndicate, 1986.
6. David Elkind, 69.
7. J. Piaget, *The Psychology of Intelligence* (London: Routledge & Kegan Paul, 1950).
8. Dolores Curran, *Traits of a Healthy Family* (New York: Ballantine Books, 1983), 247.
9. David Elkind, 9.
10. Robert Coles, "What Makes Children Grow Up Good?" An Interview conducted by Edward Wakin, *U.S. Catholic,* August 1979, 34.
11. Jay Kesler, *Too Big to Spank* (Ventura, CA: Regal Books, 1978), 83.
12. Norman Vincent Peale, "Runaway," *Guideposts Magazine,* July 1978, 11.

Chapter 3
1. Ann McCarroll, "Getting to Know Children Requires Lots of Good Talk," Christian Science Monitor News Service. Reprinted in *The Denver Post,* 19 June 1980.
2. James 3:2–6, NIV.
3. Norman Cousins, *Human Options* (New York: W. W. Norton & Company, 1981), 179.

4. James Dobson, *Parenting Isn't for Cowards* (Waco, TX: Word Books, 1987).

5. "Cat's in the Cradle," words and music by Sandy and Harry Chapin. © 1974 by Story Songs, Ltd. All rights reserved. Used by permission.

6. Dolores Curran, *Traits of a Happy Family* (New York: Ballantine Books, 1983), 40–41.

7. Lee Salk, quoted in Dolores Curran. Ibid, 63.

Chapter 4

1. Based on a classic study by Paul Rankin at Ohio State University as early as 1928 and confirmed by subsequent studies.

2. Ann McCarroll, "Getting to Know Children Requires Lots of *Good Talk,*" Christian Science Monitor News Service. Reprinted in *The Denver Post,* 19 June 1980.

Chapter 5

1. Transactional analysis was developed by Eric Berne and later popularized in Thomas Harris' book *I'm OK, You're OK*, 1967.

2. Albert Mehrabian, *Nonverbal Communication* (Chicago: Aldine Publishing Co., 1972).

3. Ecclesiastes 3:1, 7.

Chapter 6

1. Carol Tavris, *Anger* (New York: Simon & Schuster, 1982), 34.

2. Proverbs 15:1.

3. Proverbs 15:18.

4. Proverbs 29:11.

5. Proverbs 29:33.

6. Lewis B. Smedes, *Forgive & Forget* (New York: Pocket Books, 1984), 12.

7. Peter Marshall, *The Prayers of Peter Marshall* (New York: McGraw-Hill Book Company, Inc., 1949).

Chapter 7

1. Diana Baumrind, cited in Merton P. Strommen and A. Irene Strommen, *Five Cries of Parents* (San Francisco: Harper & Row, Publishers, 1985), 87–91.

2. Strommen & Strommen, 88.

3. David Elkind, *All Grown Up & No Place to Go* (Reading, MA: Addison-Wesley Publishing Co., 1984), 201.

4. Strommen & Strommen, 80.

5. Ibid., 91.

6. Ibid.

7. Ibid.

8. Bruce Narramore, *Adolescence Is Not an Illness* (Old Tappan, New Jersey: Fleming H. Revell Co., 1980), 116.

Chapter 8

1. Proverbs 16:32.

2. Practical applications of the four temperament theory have been made by Performax Systems International, Inc. through their Personal

Profile System, Leadership Dynamics International in their Personal Leadership Development programs, Tim LaHaye in his book *Your Temperament: Discover Its Potential,* and Florence Littauer in her book *Personality Plus.*

Chapter 9
1. David Elkind, *All Grown Up & No Place to Go: Teenagers In Crisis* (Reading, MA: Addison-Wesley Publishing Company, 1984), 199.
2. Parent's Music Resource Center, *Let's Talk Rock,* (Arlington, Virginia: Parent's Music Resource Center, 1986), 8.
3. "Suicidal Failure," *Suicide Tendencies,* Frontier FLP 1011. You'll Be Sorry Music. Copyright © 1983 American Legion Music, quoted in Tipper Gore, *Raising PG Kids in an X-Rated World* (Nashville: Abingdon Press, 1987), 106.
4. Suicide Solution, Ozzy Osbourne, "Suicide Solution," *Blizzard of Oz,* Jet JZ 36812. Words and Music by Ozzy Osbourne, Bob Daisky, Randy Rhodes. Jet Music Ltd. Copyright © 1981 Essex Music International Lts. TRO-Essex Music International, Inc. New York, controls all U.S.A. and Canada publication rights. Quoted in Tipper Gore, 107.
5. AC/DC, "Let Me Put My Love into You" and "Shoot to Thrill," *Back in Black,* Atlantic SD 16018. Written by Angus Young, Malcolm Young, and Brian Johnson. Published by J. Albert and Son Publishing, Lts./E.B. Marks Music. Quoted in Tipper Gore, 88.
6. Blackie Lawless, *Hit Parader,* November, 1985.
7. Motley Crue lyrics discussed on a James Dobson tape on Rock Music Lyrics, Focus on the Family, 1987.
8. "Easy Prey" lyrics discussed on a James Dobson tape, Rock Music Lyrics, Focus on the Family, 1987.
9. Georges Sulmers, "Lizzy Borden: Mock Murder Metal Rebel," *The Best of Metal Mania •1* (New York: Tempo Publishing Company. Vol 1, No. 1, 1987), 73.
10. Joe Stuessy, quoted in Tipper Gore, 120.
11. Venom, *Welcome to Hell,* Neat Records 1-002LP, lyrics discussed in Tipper Gore, 120.
12. Dann Cuellar, quoted in Tipper Gore, 123.
13. Sandi Gallant, quoted in Tipper Gore, 123.
14. Nikki Sixx, *Faces* Magazine, September 1984.
15. David Elkind, *The Hurried Child: Growing Up Too Fast Too Soon* (Reading, MA: Addison-Wesley Publishing Company, 1981), 88.
16. Dick Dutton and Brian Gleason, "It's Only Booze," *Church Herald,* 3/1/85, 11.
17. William J. Bennett, *Schools without Drugs,* United States Department of Education, 1987, V.
18. *Time,* 9/15/86, 61.
19. *Time,* 9/15/86, 68.
20. *Time,* 9/22/86, 25.
21. Charles P. Hannaford, *Germantown News,* 5 February 1987, 1.
22. Bill Cosby, *The Cosby Show.*
23. Harold M. Voth, *How to Get Your Child Off Marjuana,* Patient Care Publications, 1980.

24. Pearl Washington, "Family Ties Loosened by Addiction," *The Commercial Appeal,* 4/28/86, C2.

25. Louis Harris Poll, interviews with 1000 12–17 yr.-olds. during September/October 1986, reported in *Children & Teens Today,* April, 1987, 1.

26. David Van Bieme, "What's Gone Wrong with Teen Sex," *People,* 13 April, 1987, 11.

27. Ann Landers, *Sex and the Teenager,* Creators Syndicate, Inc., 1987.

28. Bryan E. Robinson and Robert L. Barret, "Teenage Fathers," *Psychology Today,* December 1985, 70.

29. Ibid.

30. Ibid., 67.

31. Robert L. Carl, "Out of the Darkness: The Unmarried Teen Father," *Living with Teenagers,* April, May, June, 1987, 17.

32. Byran E. Robinson & Robert L. Barret, 69.

33. Sol Gordon, "What Kids Need to Know" *Psychology Today,* October, 1986, 22.

34. Ted Koppel, *Time,* 6/22/87, 69.

35. Josh McDowell, *How to Help Your Child Say No to Sexual Pressure* (Waco, TX: Word Books, 1987), 45.

36. Richard Krawiec, *USA Today,* 3/20/87, 12A.

37. *Commercial Appeal,* 3/12/87, 2A.

38. *USA Today,* 3/20/87, 12A.

39. *Commercial Appeal,* Anita Houk, 9/22/85, B1, 2.

40. Ibid.

41. *USA Today,* 4/21/87, 5D.

42. Ibid.

43. *Focus On The Family,* 7/86, 4.

44. This prayer closes with the famous "Serenity Prayer" by Rheinhold Niebuhr.

Chapter 10
1. I disagree with all these statements.

2. Earl D. Wilson, *Try Being a Teenager* (Portland, OR: Multnomah Press, 1982), 51.

3. David Augsburger, *Caring Enough To Confront* (Ventura, CA: Regal Books, 1982), p. 11.

4. James 3:3–6.

5. Paul W. Swets, *The Art of Talking So That People Will Listen: Getting Through to Family, Friends And Business Associates* (Englewood Cliffs, New Jersey: Prentice-Hall, Inc., 1983), Chapter 10.

6. Ibid., 154.

Chapter 11
1. Graham Green quoted in Ann Rosenfeld and Elizabeth Stark, "The Prime of Our Lives," *Psychology Today,* May 1987, 63.

2. Proverbs 2:1–4.

3. Proverbs 1:7.

4. Jerald G. Bachman, "Adolescence: An Eye on the Future," *Psychology Today,* July 1987, 8.

5. See Daniel Yankelovich, *New Rules: Searching for Self-Fulfillment in a World Turned Upside Down* (New York: Random House, 1981).

6. Alexander Austin and Kenneth Green quoted in Paul Chance, "The One Who Has the Most Toys When He Dies, Wins," *Psychology Today,* 5/87, 54.

7. Venita Van Caspel, *Money Dynamics for the '80s* (Austin, TX: S & S Press, 1988), 51.

8. Matthew 6:33.

9. 1 Timothy 6:10.

10. Psalm 24:1.

11. Harry Stack Sullivan, quoted in Charlie W. Shedd, ed., *You Are Somebody Special* (New York: Mcgraw-Hill Book Co., 1982), 102.

12. Nick Stinnett and John Defrain, *Secrets of Strong Families* (Boston, MA: Little, Brown & Company, 1985).

13. Irene Kassorla "You and the Person You May Marry," Charlie Shedd, ed. *You Are Somebody Special* (New York: McGraw-Hill, 1982), 105.

14. Ann Landers, quoted in *Skills for Living* (Columbus, Ohio: A Project of the Quest National Center, 1982), 241.

15. See 1 Corinthians 6:18–20 and Exodus 20:14.

16. See Malachi 2:16 and Matthew 5:31–32.

17. *Skills for Living,* 250.

18. Allan Bloom, *The Closing of the American Mind* (New York: Simon & Schuster, 1987), 57.

19. Ibid., 57.

20. Merton and Irene Strommen, "Raising Christian Children," *The Church Herald,* 17 May 1985, 14.

21. Ibid.

22. Ibid.

23. Ibid.

24. Kenneth S. Kantzer, "Building Faith in Children," *Christianity Today,* 13 June 1986, 16.

25. Strommen, 14.

26. Proverbs 22:6.

27. The outline used here follows the outline of the gospel used by D. James Kennedy in his book *Evangelism Explosion.*

28. Ethel Leestma Swets, *Consecrated Hands* (Grand Rapids, Michigan: Zondervan Publishing House, 1956), 17.

Chapter 12
1. Victor B. Cline, *How to Make Your Child a Winner* (New York: Walker and Company, 1980), 163.

2. William Glasser, *Reality Therapy* (New York: Harper & Row, Publishers, 1965).

3. 1 Corinthians 13:4, 5, 7.

Postscript: A Word of Encouragement
1. Norman Cousins, *Human Options* (New York: W. W. Norton & Company, 1981), 68.

2. William Shakespeare, King Lear I, iv.

3. Psalm 127:3.

Resources for Parents

Claudia Arp, *Almost Thirteen: Shaping Your Child's Teenage Years Today,* Nashville: Thomas Nelson Publishers, 1986. For parents of preteens.

David Augsburger, *Caring Enough to Confront,* Ventura, CA: Regal Books, 1982. A guide on how to understand and express deep feelings.

Robert G. Barnes, Jr., *Single Parenting,* Wheaton, IL: Tyndale House Publishers Inc., 1985. Advice on how to survive loneliness, anger, and rejection, and restore family relationships.

Bethany Christian Services is a licensed child placement agency supported by Christians across the United States and Canada: 901 Eastern Ave. N.E., Grand Rapids, MI 49503-1295.

Lenore Buth, *Sexuality: God's Precious Gift to Parents and Children.* Concordia Publishing House, 1982. Tells parents how to talk to pre-adolescents and teens about sex in a straightforward and loving way.

Ross Campbell, *How to Really Love Your Teenager,* Wheaton, IL: Victor Books, 1983. How parents can let teens know they are loved and accepted.

Lawrence J. Crabb, Jr. and Dan B. Allender, *Encouragement: The Key to Caring,* Grand Rapids, MI: Zondervan Publishing House, 1984. Shows how to go beyond surface relationships and meet the emotional needs of others.

Dolores Curran, *Traits of a Healthy Family,* New York: Ballantine Books, 1983. Fifteen qualities most often found in healthy families.

Richard D. Dobbins, *Venturing into a Teenager's World,* Old Tappan, NJ: Fleming H. Revell Co., 1986. Helps parents understand what it's like to be a teenager.

James Dobson, *Dare to Discipline,* Wheaton, IL: Tyndale House Publishers, Inc., 1970. A guide for constructive, firm discipline, including natural and logical consequences.

————, *Hide or Seek,* Old Tappan, NJ: Fleming H. Revell Co., 1974. Ten strategies through which parents can cultivate self-esteem in their teenagers.

————, *The Strong-Willed Child: Birth through Adolescence,* Wheaton, IL: Tyndale House Publishers, Inc., 1978. Practical advice for parents who think they have exhausted their options.

————, *Parenting Isn't for Cowards,* Waco, TX: Word Books, 1987. Dr. Dobson's eleventh book reveals his insights gleaned from a survey of 35,000 parents about raising strong-willed and compliant youth.

David Elkind, *The Hurried Child: Growing Up Too Fast Too Soon,* Reading, MA: Addison-Wesley Publishing Co., 1981. A perceptive look at how stress affects preteenagers.

————, *All Grown Up and No Place to Go: Teenagers in Crisis,* Reading, MA: Addison-Wesley Publishing Co., 1984. Offers advice that will help parents guide their teenagers through the turbulent years of adolescence.

Tipper Gore, *Raising PG Kids in an X-Rated Society,* Nashville: Abingdon Press, 1987. Explicit review of the irresponsible excesses in the entertainment industry and steps parents can take to fight back.

Kathleen M. Gow, *Yes, Virginia, There is Right and Wrong,* Wheaton, IL: Tyndale House Publishers, Inc., 1985. A well-researched and provocative assessment of the values our teens are being taught in the public schools.

Jay Kesler, ed., *Parents & Teenagers,* Wheaton, IL: Victor Books, 1984. A comprehensive resource for parents by numerous authors.

Margie M. Lewis, *The Hurting Parent,* Grand Rapids: Zondervan Publishing House, 1980. A rare combination of restraint and honesty about how to deal with hurt in parenting.

Josh McDowell, *How to Help Your Child Say No to Sexual Pressure,* Waco, TX: Word Books, 1987. Usable insights for parents in helping their teens face tremendous pressure in today's permissive society.

Alan Loy McGinnis, *Bringing Out the Best in People,* Minneapolis: Augsburg Publishing House, 1985. Thoughts on how to help others excel.

Bruce Narramore, *Adolescence Is Not an Illness,* Old Tappan, NJ: Fleming H. Revell Co., 1980. An empathetic approach to what makes teens tick and how parents can relate to them.

Parents Music Resource Center, *Rising to the Challenge.* A video for parents describing what is going on in rock music. 1500 Arlington Blvd., Arlington, VA 22209.

Fritz Ridenour, *What Teenagers Wish Their Parents Knew about Kids,* Waco, Texas: Word Books, 1982. Focuses on parents' need to listen, respect, and trust their teens.

Arvella Schuller, *The Positive Family,* New York: A Jove Book, 1983. Inspiration and strategies to bring about positive change in the home.

Robert H. Schuller, *Power Ideas for a Happy Family,* Old Tappan, NJ: Fleming H. Revell Co., 1972. Advice for every member of the family that will motivate improved relationships in the home.

Gary Smalley, *The Key to Your Child's Heart,* Waco, TX: Word Books, 1984. Help for building a close-knit family.

Nick Stinnett and John Defrain, *Six Secrets of Strong Families,* Boston, MA: Little Brown & Co., 1985. Research-based study of healthy families.

Merton P. Strommen and A. Irene Strommen, *Five Cries of Parents,* New York: Harper & Row Publishers, 1985. A perceptive study on what troubles parents most about raising children.

Charles Stanley, *How to Keep Your Kids on Your Team,* Nashville: Oliver-Nelson, 1986. Practical ways to build strong family relationships.

Paul W. Swets, *The Art of Talking So That People Will Listen: Getting through to Family, Friends & Business Associates,* Englewood Cliffs, NJ: Prentice-Hall, Inc., 1983. An encouraging guide for establishing positive communication patterns.

U.S. Department of Education, *What Works: Schools Without Drugs,* 1987. A careful description of the effects of drug use and what parents and schools can do to fight drug use. To order a free copy, write: Schools Without Drugs, Pueblo, CO 81009.

Rich Wilkerson, *Teenagers: Parental Guidance Suggested,* Eugene, OR: Harvest House Publishers, 1983. Biblically based concepts to assist parents in helping their teenagers become mature adults.

Earl D. Wilson, *Try Being a Teenager,* Portland, OR: Multnomah Press, 1982. A challenge to parents to stay in touch with their teenagers.

Norman Wright and Rex Johnson, *Communication: Key to Your Teens,* Eugene, OR: Harvest House Publishers, 1978. Principles for making positive changes in family communication patterns.

Phyllis and David York and Ted Wachtel, *Toughlove,* New York: Bantam Books, 1983. A strong approach for dealing with drug abuse.

Zig Ziglar, *Raising Positive Kids in a Negative World,* Nashville: Thomas Nelson Publishers, 1985. Offers a positive perspective on how to raise children in difficult circumstances.

Philip Zimbardo, *The Shy Child,* New York: McGraw-Hill Book Co., 1981. Practical insights for understanding and encouraging the shy child by the Director of the Stanford Shyness Clinic at Stanford University.

Resources for Teenagers

Richard Bolles, *What Color Is Your Parachute?* Berkeley: Ten Speed Press, Current edition. A useful manual for finding a job and choosing a career.

Campus Life Magazine, Carol Stream, IL: Christianity Today, Inc. (465 Gunadersen Drive, Carol Stream, IL 60189-9828). A bright and bold magazine for junior and senior high youth.

S. Rickly Christian, *Alive,* Wheaton: Tyndale, Campus Life books. An excellent daily devotional for teens.

James Dobson, *Preparing For Adolescence,* Santa Ana, CA: Vision House Publishers, 1978. A guide to help pre-teens understand what's happening to them physically, mentally, and emotionally.

Doug Fields and Todd Temple, *Creative Dating,* Nashville, TN: Oliver Nelson, 1986. Ideas to inspire fun and fulfilling relationships.

Bill Sanders, *Tough Turf: A Teen Survival Manual,* Old Tappan, NJ: Fleming H. Revell Co., 1986. Direction for teens in dealing with self-esteem, peer pressure, and drugs.

Charlie Shedd, *The Stork Is Dead,* Waco, TX: Word Books, 1976. A book for teens that tells it like it is about sex as God meant it to be.

———, ed., *You Are Somebody Special,* New York: McGraw-Hill Book Co., 1982. A guidebook for teens written by ten authors.

Tim Stafford, *A Love Story,* Wheaton, IL: Tyndale House Publishers, 1976. An informative book on questions and answers about sex that offers Bible-based help.

The Student Bible, New International Version, Grand Rapids, MI: Zondervan Publishing House, 1986. Encourages daily Bible study by dividing the Bible into manageable portions.

For information regarding speaking engagements or seminars, write:

Dr. Paul W. Swets
1132 Longreen Dr.
Memphis, TN 38119

Index

PAUL SWETS has had extensive experience as a speaker, pastor, and seminar leader. At the University of Michigan, he earned a Doctor of Arts degree in English, with primary research in the field of rhetoric, the study of effective communication. His first book, *The Art of Talking So That People Will Listen* (Prentice-Hall, 1983), is now in its seventh printing. Dr. Swets is Minister to Families at Second Presbyterian Church in Memphis, Tennessee.

JUDSON SWETS is the president of his senior class at Ridgeway High School and was inducted into the Ridgeway Hall of Fame, an honor awarded to the top twenty seniors of his school who show outstanding leadership and scholastic ability. He has lettered in cross-country and tennis. Jud developed a survey which provides original information for his chapter on "Five Messages Teens Want to Hear." The survey supplements his own extensive reading and firsthand experience as a teenager. Jud plans to enter Wheaton College this fall and major in psychology and philosophy.